Shri Vallabh Siddhant

Synoptic Themes

An introductory text on Suddhadvaita Philosophy

Published in Great Britain by PCC Ltd,
Leicester, Leicestershire

ISBN 978-0-9563848-1-2

This book is dedicated with love and affection to the entire Modi family and in particular to the most recent additions to the family, Shyam and Kishan Modi.

Shri Jamnadas Gordhandas Modi

Late Gordhandas Govindji Modi

Smt Champaben Jamnadas Modi

Master Shyam J. Modi

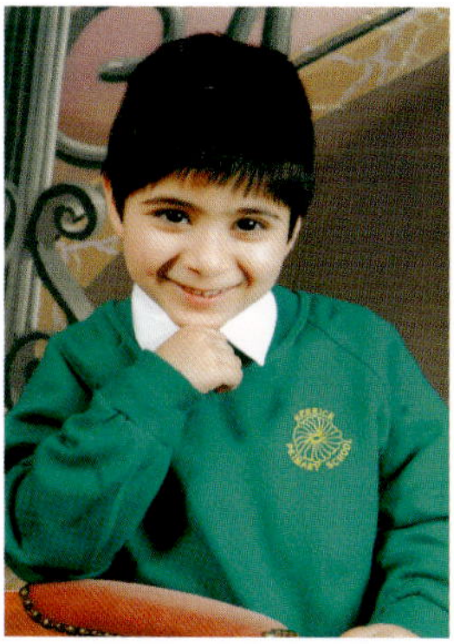

Master Kishan J. Modi

Blessings

We are honoured by the blessings wc havc rcccivcd from our parents and grandparents, as well as from the world-renowned and leading Shri Vallabh Siddhant authority, Goswami Shri Shyam Manoharlalji (Parla West, Bombay).

The following is a generous blessing given by Goswami Shri Indira Betiji, the internationally recognised and leading exponent of Shri Vallabh Siddhant.

Dr Jagdish Modi comes from a family with a long-standing tradition and deep-rooted following of Shri Vallabh Siddhant. I have personally known his parents Shri Jamnadas Gordhandas Modi and Smt Champaben Modi, themselves great practicing devotees, for many years.

I congratulate Dr Modi for writing this text, which shows many facets of Shri Vallabh Siddhant from both spiritual and devotional aspects.

The text is particularly useful for the younger generation as it provides easily accessible explanations of the fundamentals of Pusti-Marg. In this way it serves as an excellent introduction and splendid, pithy presentation of Shri Vallabh Siddhant.

I give my sincere blessing to Dr Modi and to this project.

Goswami Shri Indira Betiji
August 2007

Blessings

The following is a generous blessing given by Goswami Shri Vrajpriyji Shri Murlidharji, a great advocate of Pusti-Marg.

Shri Hari.

I am delighted to find this book *Shri Vallabh Siddhant*, by Dr. Jagdish J. Modi. It is lucid and comprehensive, and most informative about the philosophy and practical aspects of Pusti-Marg. I am confident that the fresher (newcomers to Pusti-Marg) and those already acquainted with the philosphy will definitely enjoy the blend of these two aspects of Pusti--Marg.

I have been acquainted with the Modi family since the 1980's, and personally know Dr. Jagdish Modi, his quest for spiritual knowledge, and his firm belief in the practice of Pusti-Marg, the Path of Devotion. My blessings are always with Dr. Jagdish Modi to continue his efforts in bringing out more and more writings on Shri Vallabhacharya's works and to serve the English-speaking world in better understanding the Pusti Bhakti Marg.

Goswami Shri Vrajpriyji Shri Murlidharji
Borivali [West], Mumbai
March 2010

About the Author

Dr Jagdish Modi's academic background is in Computer Science and Mathematics. He received a PhD in Computer Science from the University of London in 1982, and then subsequently joined the University of Cambridge, where he continued his research in Parallel Computing. He has written a book on parallel algorithms, published a number of research papers, as well as served as editor for several scientific journals.

In 1989 he became a founding member of an independent global financial analytical company, which has now proven to be one of the successful global providers of financial and economic analysis. He was also instrumental in the formation of a research centre, a platform to work in collaboration with academia.

As well as his work in the financial sector, he continues his student supervision for King's College, Cambridge. He is a Fellow and Chartered Mathematician of the 'Institute of Mathematics and its Application' and is also a Fellow of the 'Cambridge Philosophical Society'.

He is married and has two children, Shyam aged 8 and Kishan aged 7.

Contents

Foreword

The structure and presentation of the text is excellent – it is refreshing to see a text that incorporates many different dimensions and perspectives into a more rounded view of the Shri Vallabh Siddhant, striking many notes intellectually and spiritually. Complementing the Introductory exposition with the Biography, the Lineage, the Vartas and information on the poets really gives a sense of the broader historical perspective, and the different aspects of the whole tradition.

I particularly liked the deeper discussion of the Brahmavada and the brief portraits of the poets. Too often there is only biography and theology described - the poets give the feeling, the rasa, of the Siddhant much more effectively.

The text is extremely well written and clear in its explanations, giving an objective academic setting to each section, explaining the nature of the material, giving references, etc. This makes the presentation of the ideas, stories and poetry much more compelling.

All in all, I think this is an excellent introduction in which the spirit of Vallabhacharya's philosophy is conveyed in a very thoughtful and accessible way; it seems like a great service to all.

Dr Jessica Frasier
Oxford University
May 2007

Preface

Our family has followed the path of Pusti-Marg, at least since our great-grandparents' time, and both our grandparents: **Shri Gordhandas Govindji Modi** and **Smt Nathibai Modi**, as well as our parents: **Shri Jamnadas Gordhandas Modi** and **Smt Champaben Modi** inspired us to follow **Pusti-Marg** and the principles of Shri Vallabhacharya Mahaprabhuji. It is through their, **Shri Shyam Manoharlalji**, **Shri Indira Betiji** and **Shri Vrajpriyji Shri Murlidharji's** blessing and grace that we have produced this collection of materials.

After discussing the idea with Shyam Manoharlalji over a number of years, he encouraged us to develop this book, and will also provide on-going guidance and recommendations to develop the work further. Indeed the *Brahmavada* chapter has been taken, with his consent, almost entirely from his writings.

My father and mother have always encouraged us in following Pusti-Marg. Over the last forty years our household has been blessed by various spiritual scholars, some of them direct descendents of Shri Vallabhacharya, who, visiting from India, spent time with us and gave fine discourses so that a wider audience in England could better understand the 'Path of Grace'. In particular our house - which seemed more like a 'havali' full of 'ananda' - has been blessed with the presence of Shri Krishna Sankar Sastriji (Ahmedabad), Goswami Shri Indira Beteji (Boroda), Goswami Shri Nikungalata Beteji (Mumbai), Shri Navnitpriya Sastri (Nadiad, Gujurat), Shri Niranjan Sastri (Mumbai), Goswami Shri Vrajpriyji Shri Murlidharji (Mumbai) and Shri Shyamdas (Gokul).

In conjunction, and again through our parent's associations in India, we have also been most fortunate to meet and discuss Pusti-Marg philosophy in India with other leading acharyas such as Shri Shyam Manoharlalji (Mumbai), Shri Matureshbava (Boroda) and Shri Chinubava (Gokul). It was through contact with these great minds and proponents of Pusti--Marg that much of our interest grew and developed from an early age.

I was also very fortunate that whilst at Wolfson College, Oxford, pursuing my research in Mathematics, I came across faculty members who were well-established in the area of Indology and Sanskrit. My interest and knowledge were therefore further enhanced by association with them, as well as through attending lectures in Sanskrit at the Oriental Institute, which increased my understanding of the academic setting of Shri Vallabharcharya's philosophy. Even as early as in the 1980's I recall being pleasantly surprised to learn that the philosophy was well-established and had a rich and solid foundation and that Shri Vallabhacharya was academically regarded with high esteem being the founder of the last of the four great schools of Vaishnavism.

Our parents have clearly had a significant impact on us all, and it is their natural wish that their children, grandchildren, and future generations should maintain sanskar, satbhudhi, and continue the family's interest in Pusti-Marg. Thus, it is particularly with this thought in mind that I decided to write the present text, as a legacy for those to come, and in humble thanks to our parents whose deep generosity we can never hope to repay.

The aim and purpose of this book is to present a simplified but cohesive introduction to Pusti-Marg and the principles and life of Shri Vallabhacharya. It is directed specifically at the younger generation to provide easily accessible fundamentals of Pusti-Marg as a potential stimulus to further learning.

In order to present a rounded view of Shri Vallabhacharya's philosophy, the book firstly offers an academic perspective - with overviews of Shri Vallabhacharya's key writings, and an in-depth critique of the Brahmavada - which the reader can pursue through wider examination of the source materials and the works written upon them, many of which are cited throughout this book and listed in the *References*. Secondly the reader is presented the real-life applications and implementations of the customs and daily rituals - the practical perspective – of the present-day follower of Shri Vallabhacharya's philosophy.

The spiritual perspective is difficult to define on paper, being so personal to the individual follower - for the devotional element of belief arises from the heart - nevertheless, great effort has been made to convey the feelings that a devotee of Shri Vallabhacharya's philosophy experiences and aspires to attain. And for the purpose of understanding his philosophy, this book, of course, helps the reader understand Shri Vallabhacharya himself - his background, his experiences, his personality, his strength of character, his inspiration and deep devotion.

This book is essentially a collection of extracts from other works and a synopsis of key points upon the writings of Shri Vallabhacharya.

This book therefore, provides a short presentation of relevant subjects, and supplements it with a list of references. Starting with an *Introduction* to Pusti-Marg, we continue with the *Biography* of Shri Vallabhacharya, followed by the doctrine of *Brahmavada* - which has been taken almost entirely from Shyam Manoharlalji's writings, and then Vallabhacharya's *Lineage* – which through its personality, philosophy and poetry has presented the world with Krishna devotion for more than 500 years.

Varta, or the biographies of well-known vaishnavas such as Damodardas Harsani offers an example of the day-to-day living of a vaishnav, and the *Poetry* chapter illustrates *pusti darshan* by the eight well-known Asta-Chaap poets, and by a more recent poet, Dayaram. The section on Dayaram reflects my family's, and in particular my father's, keen interest in singing at Garbo, during festival seasons such as Navratri. He used to sing many of his Garbo in Gujarati and one of his favourite Gujarati poets was Dayaram, a firm believer and follower of Pusti-Marg. Much of Dayaram's poetry was influenced by Pusti-Marg, and even a quarter of a millennium after Shri Vallabhacharya's time, the clarity in Dayaram's poetry, which aligns itself closely to the principles of Pusti-Marg, is quite revealing. For this reason I have decided to include it alongside the great Asta-Chaap poets.

The 84 Bethaks illustrate the enormous scope of Shri Vallabacharya's travels and religious disclosures throughout India from circa AD 1490. Indeed, his followers now visit these bethaks regularly to pay him tribute.

The *Writings* chapter provides an overview of his independent wrtings and commentaries, which reveal to us his thoughts, doctrines, and the inspiration and guidance he gave to the vaishnavas. This chapter seen from a more academic perspective synthesises material from a variety of sources available from the early 20th century, when an abundance of literature, produced in sporadic bursts, became available in the public domain but not in one centralised collection. The chapter provides key references for readers to take their learning further.

The *Study Notes* explain Shri Vallabacharya's philosophy within the broader context of Indian religion. The *Glossary* provides a list of terms used throughout the book, as well as some additional definitions that may provide helpful background information to the reader. The *Index*, which collects together all occurances of key words and ideas, complements this, so the reader can explore them in context. We then conclude with a list of *References*.

There has been much debate on the various dates associated with Shri Vallabhacharya, and therefore the dates provided in this text should be taken only as a guide to illustrate the significant events in his life.

We are grateful to Shyamdas whom we have known for a number of years and who himself has dedicated his life to the teachings of *Pusti--Marg*, and written extensively upon them. We have reproduced some of his prolific translation work in this book, and provided relevant references.

We are very thankful to Shyam Manoharlalji for encouraging us with his pious blessings and for providing constructive and helpful comments. We also extend our personal thanks to Dr Jessica Frasier, Dr Nicholas Sutton, and Anuradha Dooney. We would also like to give special mention to Ms. Cheryl-Lisa Hearne and Mr. Andrew Panayi for their assistance in the preparation of this book. We are also grateful to all those that have directly and indirectly helped in this work; however, we take full responsibility for any error or omission.

JAI SHRI KRISHNA

Dr Jagdish Modi, Dr Shirish Modi, Mrs Sunilaben Lakhani and family
December 2010

Shri Vallabh Siddhant

Synoptic Themes

by

Dr Jagdish J. Modi **Ph.D, FIMA, CMath**

Chapter One

Introduction

Pusti-Marg The Path of Grace

This book collects together some key fundamentals, which help to explain the concept of 'Pusti-Marg,' also known as the Brahmavada or Suddhadvaita philosophy.

In India, between the 12th and 16th centuries, four great schools of Vaishnavism arose. The schools take the names of their founders: Ramanujacharya, Madhvacharya, Nimbarkacharya and Vallabhacharya. This book is uniquely focused upon the life, works, personality, spirituality and philosophy of the last of the four, namely Shri Vallabhacharya.

Today, many people throughout India and across the world follow Shri Vallabhacharya's philosophy, which is the Philosophy of Suddhadvaita, "Pure Non-Dualism", or the "Pusti-Marg", which means "path of grace" (marg standing for path and pusti for grace). Shri Vallabhacharya was an advocate of the Brahmavada or the Suddhadvaita, and the greatest devotee of Lord Krishna. His philosophy is also sometimes known as the "Nirguna Bhakti Marg" or the "path of selfless love" towards the Lord Krishna.

Shri Vallabhacharya taught that the means of showing devotion and the rewards gained from it are the same thing; the "path of grace" sees everything as Krishna, and nothing but Krishna, so the result is always a universal truth – Krishna. Lord Krishna is sometimes referred to by other names; he is described as Brahman in the Upanishads, as

Parmatma in the Smritis, and Bhagwan in the Shrimad Bhagvatam.

Brahma Sambandh

Once, when Shri Vallabhacharya was in the sacred town of Gokul, Lord Krishna appeared and instructed him to initiate divine souls into the Pusti-Marg by means of the 'Brahma Sambhandh', an initiation ceremony. From that point onwards, only the descendants of Shri Vallabhacharya have been entitled to give Brahma Sambhandh. All those who take Brahma Sambhandh will have all impurities removed from their body and soul. Through this initiation a devotee dedicates himself, together with all his belongings and relationships, to Shri Krishna. Forever after, the devotee will then perform a daily worship of "Thakorji", the Lord. (For Brahma Sambhandh refer also to the *Glossary* chapter)

Characteristics and Devotion of the Pusti Vaishnava

Tilaka, Mudra, Cakra-Gada-Sankha-Padma and the Tulasi-mala are the traditional external marks of the Pusti Vaishnava (devotee). Firm faith and sole refuge in Shri Krishna, devotional sentiment, and the initiation of the surrender are the internal characteristics. The vaishnava's primary objective is the divine 'seva' of Shri Krishna, and the single intention in the devotee's mind is to have Shri Krishna's darshan. (For Darshan see later and refer also to the *Glossary* chapter).

'Seva' is the name for a devotional practice carried out in the home. Shri Vallabhacharya teaches that 'seva' is the highest ideal for the followers of Pusti-Marg and it is the devotee's duty to honour Shri Krishna both as the Lord of Gokul, and also as a member of one's own household. Shri Krishna should always be served with bhava and an unconditional loving attitude, whilst remembering that we are the 'sevak' or 'servant' of Lord Krishna. There are three kinds of services (seva): physical, material and mental. The latter being the most difficult to attain.

"Bhakti" or "devotion/love" that is an attitude or feeling of the heart, assumes four different forms: Tamasik, Rajasik, Sattvic and Nirguna. Pusti-Marg or Nirguna Bhakti Marg is bhakti without any object in view and without any desire but accompanied by love (nirguna). Shri

Vallabhacharya established and taught this philosophy, which requires rendering divine service to Lord Krishna, consciously and with pure heart, without any intention of reward or fruits.

Devotional routine in the Pusti-Marg is symbolised by the *eight darshan* of the day. These eight darshan are based around the divine child's day as it was in Vrindavan. Every darshan has a different bhava (deep feeling) associated with it. In order, the eight darshan of the day are: *Mangla, Sringhar, Gwala, Rajbhog, Uttaphan, Bhog, Sandhya and Sen*.

Of the eight, three: *Sringhar, Rajbhog, and Sandhya* attract a large number of people because of the time of day when they take place, respectively at 8am, noon, and in the evening. Men, women and children attend the darshan to have sight of Thakorji. The clothes, food, environment all vary daily and are appropriate to the season, with the sole aim of encouraging thoughts of Krishna lila. (For further details see Parekh, Manilal C. [reference 30])

The 'path of grace' inspires us to worship Shri Krishna as described in the Shrimad Bhagvatam, and is demonstrated by the various "playful" activities – *lilas* – exercised by Shri Krishna. Krishna eternally performs his lila or 'play' activities for his own amusement, as a game, to enjoy himself. The term lila is frequently used in literature and covers all types of Krishna's play: his eternal lila – showing and concealing parts of himself to give an illusion of change; his brajlila – playful activities in braja, his ballila – playful activities in his childhood, and his raslila – when he performs the rasa dance. He performs the lilas at different places taking on different forms at the same time. Every Vraj Gopi feels that Shri Krishna was with her, while the cowherd lads saw Krishna as their friend, every Vaishnava feels the presence of Shri Krishna. Only Shri Krishna is capable of performing the various lilas. He is described as 'Thakorji' in Pusti-Marg.

Sustained following of Pusti-Marg

The sustained following of Shri Vallabhacharya's philosophy by today's devotees worldwide is a continuation of an almost five hundred year tradition. Since the 16th century a wide spectrum of society including Rajas (Kings) in various territories, have followed the Pusti-Marg. There is also a huge following in the Indian state of Gujarat that dates back many generations. Indeed, the great Mahatma Gandhi, was himself born in the coastal city of Porbandar in the state of Gujurat and whose family observed the Pusti-Marg philosophy, and practised the household seva tradition.

Chapter Two

Biography (*)

The life of Shri Vallabhacharya

Shri Vallabhacharya lived during the period of Vikram Savant in the 16th century, at a time when political and social circumstances were far from ideal.

His ancestors came from Andhra Pradesh in India and were highly religious and learned. One of his ancestors, Yagnanarayana Bhatt, performed many Vedic Somyagnas. His devotion was so great that when he was performing Somyagna, Lord Krishna himself proclaimed that he would appear in his family upon the completion of the hundredth Somyagna, in order to protect and spread religious knowledge. These were peformed by Shri Vallabhacharya's ancestors as illustrated with the chart on page twenty.

Birth of Vallabhacharya

Shri Vallabhacharya was born in 1535 (AD 1479), in Champaranya, India, the son of Laksman Bhatt and Illmagaaru. During his childhood he began taking an interest in religious debates with Pandits and Sanyasis.

In 1540, at the early age of five, Vallabhacharya started to study during Vikram Savant in the greatly celebrated month of Chaitra. In the same year he studied and stayed with his Guruji Shri Vishnuchit, from whom he learned *Yajur Veda*. He also learned *Rug Veda* and *Sam Veda* from Acharya Tirumal;

(*) Extracts in this chapter have been taken from Parekh, Lallubhai Pranvallabhadas [reference 28] & Shah, Natvarlal Gokaldas [reference 38].

Krishna Yajur Veda from his father; *Paniniysutra, Astodyayi, Gautam, Yog, Sankhaya, Mimamsa, Agam* and so on from Acharya Narayan Dixit; and finally *Bhagvad-Gita, Shrimad Bhagvatam and Narad Panchtatva* from Acharya Madhavendrayati.

A short time after the completion of his studies, his father died in the holy place of Kashi, in Samvat 1546 (AD 1490). Shri Vallabhacharya was just eleven years old and had two brothers and two sisters. Soon after, he left Kashi and headed south on a pilgrimage.

When Shri Vallabhacharya reached Shukarshetra, Krishnadas Meghan, a well-known vaishnava, surrendered himself to him and decided to join Shri Vallabhacharya and his disciples, who then travelled to Pampa Sarovar.

During the pilgrimage (refer to *The 84 Bethaks* chapter) Vallabhacharya went to different places, performing a yagan of Ved and Bhagavat Parayan. His main intention was to spread religious knowledge and enlighten others to the Krishna lila. It was at this time that he founded the school of bhakti, the Pusti-Marg - the path of acquiring grace of Lord Krishna. Pusti vaishnavas, those who follow the Pusti-Marg, proclaimed Shri Vallabhacharya "Shri Mahaprabhuji", because of his greatness.

Vallabhacharya went to Vaikunthkshetra, where he taught the four different forms (gunas) of bhakti, namely, *Tamasik, Rajasik, Sattvic and Nirguna*. He particularly emphasised *Nirguna bhakti* – or loving the divine form without expecting fruits in return. Nirguna bhakti does not mean without attribute, but it means that which is beyond the influence of the three gunas, arising from Prakruti or Maya, namely Sattvic, Rajas and Tamas.

During his lifetime Vallabhacharya undertook three pilgrimages throughout India to teach his unconditional devotion to Shri Krishna. He dedicated his life to the religious and moral fulfilment of society.

Following the order of Shri Krishna, Vallabhacharya initiated his disciples with *'Brahma Sambhandh'*, and preached that the 'seva' of Shri Krishna is the duty of the vaishnava. He emphasised seva as a household lineage, describing three types of seva, namely physical, material and mental. (For Brahma Sambhandh refer also to the *Introduction* and *Glossary*)

The Composition of Shri Yamunashtak

On one occasion Shri Vallabhacharya went with his sevaks to Gokul, a desolate place with neither house nor human being to be seen anywhere. Whilst in a large forest he explained to his sevaks, that it was in this very place that Lord Krishna performed his childhood lilas. When they crossed the Yamuna river, Shri Yamunaji appeared to them. It was here, at the age of fourteen, that Shri Vallabhacharya sang the famous *Yamunashtak* as a eulogy to Shri Yamunaji.

Shri Vallabhacharya was one of the greatest philosophers of India, and also an illustrious advocate of the Brahmavada or the Suddhadvaita. The following is a short summary of the main features and teachings of his life.

1. Aged five, Shri Vallabhacharya started his studies with Guru Shri Vishnuchit.

2. When he was eleven and had just finished his studies, Vallabhacharya's father died in Kashi, in Samvat 1546 (AD 1490).

3. Following his father's death he went on a pilgrimage and at the age of thirteen established the Doctrine of Brahmavada.

4. Shri Vallabhacharya founded the Pusti-Marg and explained the importance of Nirguna Bhakti. His advice to the vaishnavas was: -

    (a) God, the absolute being, is truth. He takes a Form or a Shape. He is absolute bliss. He is Omnipresent.

    (b) The vaishnava should always try to conquer mental enemies such as passion, anger and greed.

    (c) The vaishnava should have a pure love for and attachment to God, and all his activities should be exclusively confined to the service of God.

    (d) God accepts nothing other than selfless love.

5. He preached the seva of Shri Krishna as the highest ideal of the vaishnava.

6. He treated his disciples with love and respect and guided them.

7. During his journey, he performed the parayan of Shrimad Bhagvatam in the majority of the 84 places that he visited.

8. Following the order from Shri Krishna, he initiated his disciples with Brahma Sambhandh through self-renunciation and gave to each one a deity of Lord Krishna in the form of "Thakorji" and taught them to perform the seva.

9. He completed his first pilgrimage through India in Vikram Samvat 1554, in the month of Vaishakh.

10. Before long, he started his second pilgrimage in Vikram Samvat 1555, in the month of Chaitra. After five years he completed his second pilgrimage.

11. Soon after he married Mahalaxmi, daughter of Dev Bhatt.

12. Six months after his marriage, he embarked upon his third pilgrimage, which was completed in four years.

13. When Vallabhacharya returned from Dwarka and Jagannath, he was inspired by God to conclude his missionary work and retire to his abode. But at that time his work upon the 'Subodhiniji' text was still incomplete.

14. Shortly after, he entered 'Madhuvan' near Mathura. He was again reminded by God to end his missionary work on earth. Again the work on 'Subodhiniji' delayed him.

15. When he went to Adel, God asked him to retire for the third time. This time he could not resist. Subsequently he composed the 'Antah-Karana-Prabodha' text and read it to his wife and other relatives to console them.

16. Finally he went to Kashi on Hanuman ghat and plunged himself in the holy waters of the Ganges, on Sunday the third day Ashadha month, in Samvat 1587 (AD 1531).

17. His noblest contribution was in the extension of Brahmavada, popularly known as Suddhadvaita-pure nondualism, and also his "Subodhiniji" critique on several parts of the Shrimad Bhagvatam Puran and various other literary original works.

18. His compositions can be classified under two headings:

(a) *Independent writings*, of which there are twenty-five:

> (1) Yamunashtak (2) Siddhantamuktavali (3) Pusti-Pravaha-Maryada (4) Balabodha (5) Siddhanta Rahasyam (6) Navratna (7) Antah-Karana-Prabodha (8) Viveka-Dhairya-Asraya (9) Chatussloki (10) Krishnasraya (11) Bhaktivardhini (12) Panchapadyani (13) Jalabheda (14) Sanyasanirnaya (15) Nirodha-Lakshanani (16) Sevaphalam.

This first group of sixteen is known as 'Shodas Grantha'. The remaining writings are:

> (17) Sanyas Vidhi (18) Madhurashtaka (19) Shri Parivrithashtaka (20) Trividha Namavali (21) Purushottam Sahasra Namani (22) Nyasadesh (23) Patravalambana (24) Tattva-Dipa-Nibandha (25) Shiksha-Shloka.

(b) *Commentary works*, which are:

> (1) Purva Mimamsa Bhasya or Jaimini Sutra Bhasya (2) Uttar Mimamsa Bhasya or Brahmasutranubhasya or Anubhasya (3) Shri Subodhini (4) Sukshma Tika upon Shrimad Bhagvatam (5) 'Prakash' the commentary on Tatwartha.

A synopsis of many of these works is provided in the *Writings* chapter.

The following time-line illustrates significant dates and events in Shri Vallabhacharya's life.

Time-line highlighting the key aspects of Shri Vallabhacharya's life

VS: Vikram Samvat

1535 | 1540 | 1545 | 1550 | 1555 | 1560 | 1565 | 1570 | 1575 | 1580 | 1585 | 1590

Shri Vallabhacharya born in VS 1535 (AD 1479).

At the early age of five, in VS 1540, Shri Vallabhacharya began his studies.

When Shri Vallabhacharya was 11, his father died in Kashi, in VS 1546 (AD 1490).

First Pilgrimage (VS 1546 - 1554)

The first tour was to South India, to spread religion in the form of Krishna Lila. During each of the three pilgrimages, Shri Vallabhacharya performed the parayan of Shrimad Bagavatam in the majority of the 84 places he visited.

Brahma Sambhandh

On the 11th day of the bright half moon of Shravana month, Shri Vallabhacharya arrived in Gokul. During the night Shri Krishna instructed Shri Vallabhacharya to initiate his disciples with Brahma Sambhandh through self-renunciation. He completed his first pilgrimage in VS 1554 in the month of Vaishakh.

Second Pilgrimage (VS 1555 - 1560)

Shri Vallabhacharya started his second tour on the 2nd day of the bright half of Chaitra, VS 1555. The second tour was to the Northern and Eastern parts of India. Shri Vallabhacharya married Mahalaxmi, daughter of Dev Bhatt.

Third pilgrimage (VS 1561 - 1565)

His third tour lasted 4 years. He revisited some of the places from his first and second pilgrimages. He decided to settle in Banaras, one of the greatest learning centres in all of India.

Inspired by Lord Krishna to end his missionary work on earth, and retire to his abode.

Since the Subodhiniji text was incomplete, only after the third request did he decide to retire to his abode. He composed the 'Antah-Karana-Prabodha' to console his wife and relatives.

On the 3rd day of the bright half of Ashad, in VS 1587, Shri Vallabhacharya plunged into the holy waters of the Ganges.

A brilliant flame in the form of God arose from the waters and took him away.

His <u>noblest contributions</u> were the extension of Brahmavada, known as Suddhadvaita Pure Non-Dualism, and the 'Subodhiniji', critique on Shrimad Bhagvatam

NOTE: *Although the author has attempted to provide a general framework on the time-line, it should be noted that there was much debate on the birth-date of Shri Vallabhacharya, see, for example, late Prof. G.H. Bhatt (1984), and therefore the time-line provided should be taken as a guideline only, to illustrate the relative order of significant events in Shri Vallabhacharya's life.*

Chapter Three

Brahmavada

The Suddhadvaita philosophy

Undoubtedly over the last 500 years there have been a number of interpretations of the Brahmavada. Below, we have chosen, almost entirely, the writings of *Goswami Shri Shyam Manohar* [reference 40, pp (vi) to (x)] as a particularly insightful perspective of this subtle and much-debated text. (Since we have reproduced his writings intact, some spellings of terms may vary slightly.)

All the mundane phenomena are the transcendental supreme self. He, the Supreme Being, is the creator and He creates Himself only. He, the Supreme Self, is the sustainer and He sustains Himself only. He, the Supreme Lord, is the destroyer and He destroys Himself only (1).

Whenever, however, wherever, by or through whatever, out of whatever, for whatever, of whatever, to whatever; in the material form or conscious form or divine form, whatever happens-it is all in all the Lord Himself (2).

The above quoted two passages sound like a poetry, but they are not written merely to give an expression to a devotional imagination of a poet. Rather they should be regarded as a great poem that strives to synthesise the different intellectual philosophies that bewilder our mind with mutual contradictions. And this synthesis too is not a subterfuge to subjugate or unfold the other systems of philosophy, into one's own system of thought, for making a claim of being all-encompassing universal philosophy.

These two passages are from the writings of Mahaprabhu Shri Vallabhacharya, the revivalist of the Shuddhadvaita Brahmavada system of Vedanta. Mahaprabhu's sole interest in this framework of philosophical system lies in its usefulness to meet the demand of devotion par excellence for the Lord Krishna. According to Mahaprabhu, this devotion is neither merely a divine relishment of the godhood of Krishna nor is it merely a realisation of the all-pervasive powers or attributes of the Brahman.

For Mahaprabhu, Krishna is both a divine person as well as an omnificent-omnipresent-omniscient and omnipotent power. Therefore, according to Mahaprabhu, an ideal devotee has to relish Brahman as Krishna and realise Krishna as Brahman (3).

Mahaprabhu says- "This world is to be realised as a part or a form of God but it should not be relished as God (4)."

We, certainly, cannot relish any single musical note but any two musical notes of mutually contradictory sounds indeed come into a charming harmony in a sweet song!

For Mahaprabhu, Krishna is both; transcendental and immanent too. He is the supreme Being Consciousness and bliss. He is all-pervasive; therefore the system of Suddhadvaita Vedanta is also a pursuit of understanding how his all-pervasive unity encompasses all the possible phenomena proposed by the other systems of thought. They are supposed as either power or form identical with the essence of the Supreme Being (5).

Yes, the God is all-pervasive; therefore, in every vision of divinity, some divine perspective is present (6).

According to some thinkers, though the two tracks of train never truly converge, yet the law of perspective produces such subjective feelings within us. Thus what we see is merely an illusion and the said law amply proves the ultimate falsity of visual experience.

As a matter of fact, in spite of the absence of any mental, subjective or cognitive activity, the law of perspective maintains it's own objective validity. This is adequately supported by the photographic reproduction of any landscape by a camera, which does not posses mind. Therefore, truly speaking, the so-called law of perspective is not so much concerned with how do we perceive, but how a visual object appears in spatial relation with the other objects. Because the visual object appears exactly in similar fashion before both: the eyes of conscious being as well as the lens of lifeless camera. This takes us for considering one more important issue of the Kantian duality between 'the thing as it is' and 'the thing as it appears'.

Here, according to different Vedantic theories viz. Vivartavada, Vikrta-parinamavada and Avikrta-parinamavada, we get the different solutions.

The kevaladvaitins propose Vivartavada. Therefore according to it, Adhisthana i.e. 'the thing as it is' is absolutely one: [A and not- (not-A)]. Thus 'the thing as it appears' is a false appearance, as the serpent falsely appears on the rope due to darkness, resemblance and the fear of serpent in person who perceives it.

The other possibility is of Vikrta-parinamavada. According to it, 'the thing as it is' e.g. milk, after being modified as curd, truly appears to be curd. But after the modification i.e., from milk to curd, if someone misconstrues the curd as milk, nobody would admit such consideration as valid knowledge.

Therefore Mahaprabhu proposes a different theory of Avikrta-parinamavada, wherein substance and its modifications are identical with each other, as in the philosophy of Spinoza. Therefore 'the thing as it is' is unknowable in manner of 'the thing as it appears', before it is modified in that particular form. But if in the process of modification, the essential identity is not lost, then the relation between 'the thing as it is' and 'the thing as it appears' cannot be defined in terms of [A & not -(not-A)], but it has to be defined in terms (A=B). Here 'A' stands for 'the thing as it is' & 'B' stands for 'the thing as it appears'.

Mahaprabhu supports his theory by giving the example of the gold and the necklace made of it. To give a little clear explanation, we can also think of an antique statue made of gold. To an ignorant gold thief, it may appear simply as gold and to a historian as an antique of much higher value than a mere piece of gold. Neither of these two appearances can be explained away in terms Adhisthan & Vivarta. Therefore the relation that subsists between the substance gold & the antique statue cannot be explained in terms of considering the gold as a real substance as false modification.

Thus the Brahman, before being modified as the world is unknowable-indescribable 'the thing as it is' in very Kantian fashion. But after being modified as the world; as gold is modified into the form of an antique or an ornament, it really becomes the world knowable as well as describable. The Brahman becomes the world without losing its essential identity. Therefore 'the thing as it is' viz. Brahman is identical with the 'the thing as it appears' viz. the world.

According to Kevaladvaitins, it can be argued that an absolutely real thing can never undergo the process of any changes. But we have to consider the whole issue more carefully.

For the sake of argument, think of any object that is merely phenomenally real, with all of its changes also being of same nature, e.g. the transformation of milk into curd. Here the milk as well as it's transformation both are phenomenally real. So there is no need to degrade the changes to the scale lower than that of the substance, which undergoes the transformation. It is not the case here that the milk is nominally real while it's transformation into curd is phenomenally real. Nor can milk be regarded as phenomenally real while the curd as mere false appearance. A question of temporal distinction can be brought into notice for emphasising the duality between the milk as it was and the milk as it, after the changing into form of curd, appears. In such a case, we would like to propose to concentrate upon the nature of the quantum theory: light is both a wave as well as a particle. Here in this case, what can be regarded as the light as it is and the light as it appears?

Therefore it is inevitable here to make one more distinction as to between what 'the thing as it is' is & what 'the human logic demands the thing to be' is.

The laws of thought are the prime necessity for any intellectual thinking;

but can our intellect be regarded as the sole criterion of objective reality? We certainly cannot intellectually grasp how something being a wave can be a particle too. We have simply to observe or presume how the light behaves surrationally! Mahaprabhu Shri Vallabhacharya considers Brahman also a supra-rational phenomenon i.e. neither rational nor irrational one.

Mahaprabhu emphatically clarifies that Brahman is all; therefore it is full of mutually contradictory attributes. Such phenomenon can sometimes be misunderstood as irrational concept, but this is merely a blind faith in reason. As a matter of fact, Brahman is supra-rational phenomenon; therefore, all philosophies can be regarded as describing some partial truth of Brahman. At the same time, no philosophy can be a total description of the totality of the truth (7).

Mahaprabhu, therefore, also confirms that any absolutistic claim of any philosophy is bound to be absolutely false. Yet even in this respect, Mahaprabhu's opinion is that even such absolutely false approach is ultimately caused or inspired by the God Himself, nay never by Satan!

Mahaprabhu says- "Although all the understandings i.e. philosophies are caused or inspired by the God but the thinkers, due to ignorance of the God, uphold their respective systems of thought as the full and final description of the ultimate reality. Some think there is no God, others think actions or rituals alone are God, some consider Him as 'mere creator' while others consider Him nothing else than their own selves. These totalistic claims are prevalent others due to ignorance and total reliance upon their own hypotheses (8)." This means that there is some truth in every theory of different systems of thought.

In brief, this is the approach of Mahaprabhu Shri Vallabhacharya's philosophy. It is very unlike the approach of Sunyavadins who say that the theory of Sunya is not to uphold the Sunya as the ultimate reality, but to get rid of all the theories, including itself about the ultimate reality. Mahaprabhu upholds the theory of Brahmavada not to falsify other theories, least can it be said to be for self-denial. For Mahaprabhu, Brahman is full of contradictory attributes; therefore all the contradictory theories are partially true including his own theory of

Suddhadvaita Brahmavada.

****

1. From Sarvanirnaya Nibandha of Mahaprabhu Sri Vallabhacharya: "Aatmaiv tadidam sarva...hastishawarah."
2. From Sastrarth Nibandha of Mahaprabhu: "Yatrayen ...pradhanpurusheshwarah."
3. Sastrartha: "Mahatmyayanpurvastu ...sneho bhaktiha."
4. From Subhodhini by Mahaprabhu: "Brahmaroopam jagad ...na tatrasaktiha."
5. Siddhantamuktavali by Mahaprabhu: "Param brahma tu Krishna...shrutemtam."
6. Subhodhini
7. Sastrartha: "Ekeko deva.... anusarti."
8. Subhodhini

Chapter Four

Lineage

Antecedents and descendents of Shri Vallabhacharya

The ancestors of Shri Vallabhacharya were the Telugu Brahmins of Andhra Pradesh, in southern India. The family belongs to the Bharadwaj Gotra of the Taitriya branch of Yajur Veda (refer to the *Study Notes* chapter). Shri Vallabhacharya was in the 8th generation descended from Shri Govindacharya. In chronological order these generations are Shri Govindacharya, Shri Vallabh Dixit, Shri Yagnanarayana Bhatt, Gangadhar Somyaji, Ganpati Bhatt, Vallabh or Bal Bhatt, Laksman Bhatt and Shri Vallabhacharya.

Shri Vallabhacharya

The family's devotion to religious learning is evident throughout the seven previous generations, and thus Shri Vallabhacharya followed strong learned ancestors with deep affection to Vaishnavism. During his childhood Shri Vallabhacharya was known amongst his teachers for his proficiency in learning and acute intelligence, who mastered during a very short period of time, the Vedas and the six systems of Hindu philosophy, the Shrimad Bhagvatam, the Bhagvad-Gita, the Bhagavad Puranas, and the Narad Panchtatva (refer to the *Biography* chapter).

Shri Gopinathji

Shri Vitthalnathji

Shri Vallabhacharya had two sons, the elder called Gopinathji and the younger Vitthalnathji. Gopinathji had two daughters and one son, Purusottamji who died at an early age. The second son, Vitthalnathji (Gosainji), had six sons and four daughters by his first wife and one son by his second wife.

Shri Hariraiji

Shri Gokulnathji

The lineage has thus continued through Vitthalnathji's seven sons: Girdharji, Govindraiji, Balkrishnaji, Gokulnathji, Raghunathji, Yadunathji and Ghanshyamji, who all continued the tradition of teaching and most importantly the initiation into the Pusti-Marg. The followers of Pusti-Marg believe in these seven descendants.

Gokulnathji had a very good following that included great scholars such as Kalyana Bhatta, the author of Rasikaranjani, an unpublished commentary in Sanskrit on the Bhagvad-Gita.

Shri Hariraiji, the illustrious son of Shri Kalyanraiji and grandson of Govindraiji, was born in Gokul in AD 1647. He was a prodigious writer, and authoritative figure in Pusti-Marg, and became known as Mahaprabhuji. He received initiation from Shri Gokulnathji at the age of eight, and learnt the seva and teachings of the Pusti-Marg from him. He later moved to Kimnor, just on the outskirts of Nathdvara, in Rajasthan. He lived for 125 years, and grace-filled the world over with devotional literature. In particular he wrote the famous Shiksha Patra, consisting of 41 letters to his brother Gopeshwar, These hold the essence of Pusti--Marg, and are recited daily by thousandas of followers. He also wrote commentary on the 84 and 252 Vaishnavas cementing the fundamentals of Pusti Marg (refer to the *Varta* chapter). His writings consisted not only in Braja Bhasa, but also in Gujarati, Maravadi, Punjabi and Sanskrit.

There are over 150 other lineage holders all of whom are direct descendants of Shri Vallabhacharya. The current head of the lineage is the Tilkayat at Nathdwara. His seat is in direct succession from Shri Vithalnathji's oldest son, Shri Girdharji. The other main seats of the Vallabhacharya tradition are in Gokul, Banaras (in Uttar Pradesh), Nathdwara, Kamvan, Kankroli (Rajasthan) and in Baroda and Surat (Gujurat).

In the Vallabharcharya lineage we see enlightened beings and their enormous contribution to the bhakti teachings through their grace-filled lifestyles.

The lineage-holders initiate followers into Pusti-Marg via Brahma Sambhandh. Thereafter the devotees will forever perform daily Krishna seva in their homes. Today there are countless followers of Pusti-Marg throughout the world, all performing daily seva of Shri Krishna. The lineage-holders themselves are well-versed in the Vedanta-Sutras philosophy, and many are also well-versed in areas such as poetry and music, but Krishna seva remains at the heart of their activity, and provides discourses into the bhakti teaching, in accordance with the teachings of Shri Vallabhacharya, to followers the world over.

Further details on Vallabhacharya's lineage can be found in Shyamdas [reference 47], Shah, J.G. [reference 37] and Parekh, Manilal C [reference 30].

The following two diagrams illustrate the ancestry and lineage of Shri Vallabhacharya and those of his descendants who contributed significantly to the proliferation of Pusti-Marg.

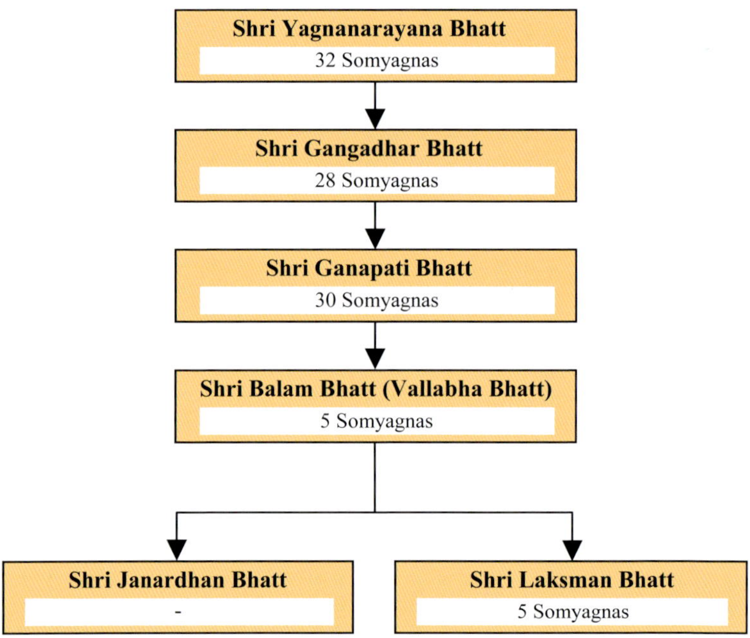

The ancestors of Shri Vallabhacharya - who performed 100 Somyagnas

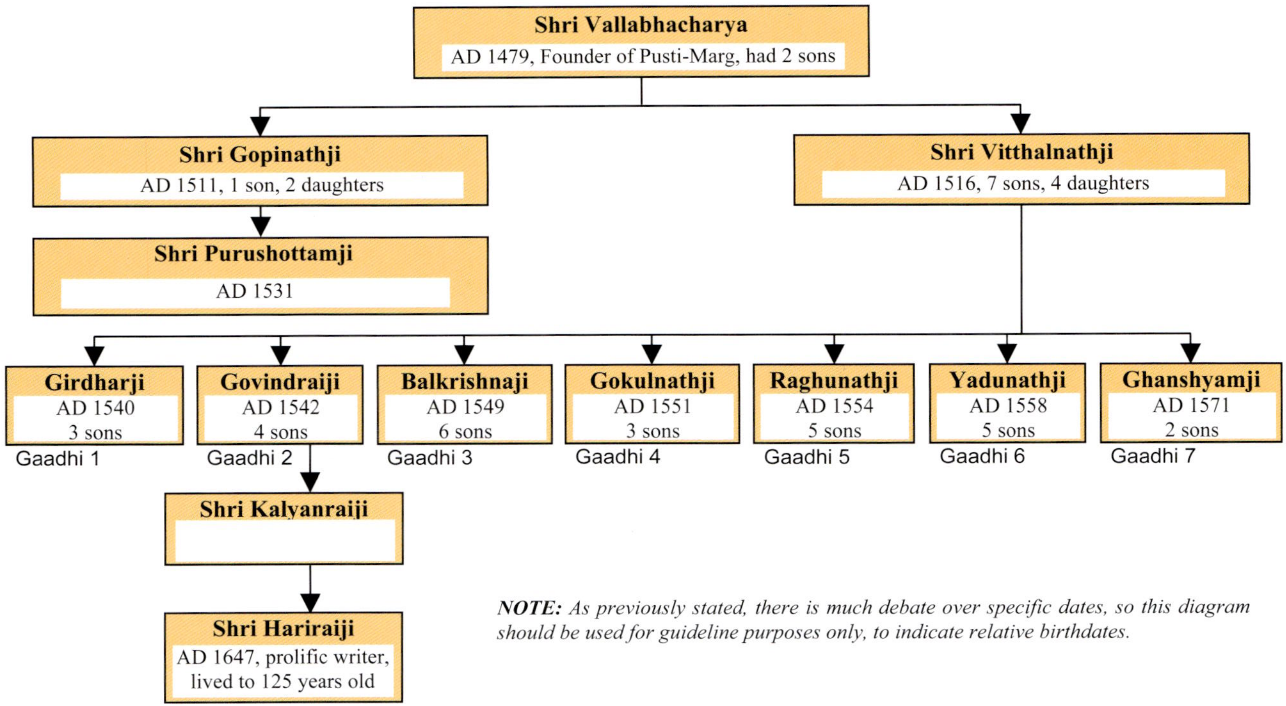

NOTE: *As previously stated, there is much debate over specific dates, so this diagram should be used for guideline purposes only, to indicate relative birthdates.*

Genealogical Tree of Shri Vallabhacharya's descendants who contributed significantly to the Pusti-Marg

Chapter Five

Varta (*)

Biographical accounts of the disciples

Shri Vallabhacharya initiated countless disciples into Pusti-Marg. Many of these disciples (vaishnavas) have themselves become well known for their devotion, poetry and vartas. Vartas are not stories, but rather biographical accounts of certain vaishnavas, and they provide detailed examples of everyday living. They also reveal the capability, reach and relevance of Shri Vallabhacharya's teachings, his practice of seva and the ways to achieve self-surrender. The vartas show how the dedicated vaishnavas performed their pure-hearted daily devotions and seva. At any stage in their lives, difficult or easy, the vartas show how they achieved and maintained *alokik lila* and happiness, both through seva and their devotional practice from association with the Bal Krishna deity.

Even today, the varta of the lives of the vaishnavas give us practical examples to follow. By studying these devotees we can easily understand the teachings and principles of Shri Vallabhacharya, for a wide range of different groups, religions and castes, coming from a variety of educational and social backgrounds, is represented in the vartas, but despite their diverse backgrounds they all adopted and lived according to the principles of Shri Vallabhacharya's Pusti-Marg. This is why the varta are so very important – they show the practical application of Pusti-Marg devotion by the devotee who has learnt and understood the principles of the

(*) Extracts in this chapter have been taken from Shyamdas [reference 46].

philosophy and has chosen to live his life in adherence to those principles.

Varta of 84 Vaishnavas

Shri Gosainji, son of Shri Vallabhacharya, handed down the varta of the '84 Vaishnavas' to Shri Gokulnathji, grandson of Shri Vallabhacharya. From amongst countless devotees, Shri Vallabhacharya personally knew the '84 Vaishnavas' who themselves became well known throughout the land. Shri Gokulnathji recited the vartas in the presence of his own disciples who in turn compiled them. The '84 Vaishnavas' are part of Shri Vallabhacharya's own divine form, they are predominantly *nirguna*, beyond material qualities.

As stated, the vartas disclose the lives and experiences of many different sections of society as well as providing a biography of the '84 Vaishnavas' and illustrating the principles of Pusti-Marg. Shri Hariraiji the illustrious descendant of Shri Vallabhacharya and disciple of Shri Gokulnathji, wrote the Bhava Prakash, which enables us to understand the lives of the vaishnavas to a deeper extent. In particular he sheds light onto the emotional state of being of the vaishnava, and in some cases the *adhibhautika* lives of a bhakta before their Brahma Sambhandh initiation, and *adhidaivika* identities of the same bhakta when they are in the divine lila in Goloka.

Shri Hariraiji's work identified the characteristics of Pusti-Marg. A number of these essential qualities are listed below and give further insight into the life of a devotee. These characteristicts are clearly observed in the lives of the '84 Vaishnavas'.

> *'Where the absence of all means is the means to achieve the fruit and where the fruit (Lord Krishna) is the means, know that to be the Blessed Path of Grace.*
>
> *Where the lord accepts the soul, does not consider its qualification, etc, nor does he delay, know that to be the Blessed Path of Grace.*
>
> *Where there is no consideration of virtue or defect, Where there is a constant feeling of appreciation in all the Lord's deed's, know that to be the Blessed Path of Grace.*

Where there is not an infinitesimal reason for the Lord's selection of the soul, but where the devotee depends solely upon His divine sweet will, know that to be the Blessed Path of Grace.

Where the relationship is both the means and achievement and is established according to Krishna's sweet will, know that to be the Blessed Path of Grace.

Where humility is the singular means for the lord's manifestation and the humility aroused in separation is the fruit, know that to be Blessed Path of Grace.

Where thought is never given to worldly and scriptural satisfaction, but only to please the Lord, know that to be the Blessed Path of Grace.

Where a devotee who has understood the intentions of scriptural injunction, remaining attached to the Lord Himself, having no obsession for scriptural duty, know that to be the Blessed Path of Grace.

In many examples of the '84 Vaishnavas' we see that in addition to having deep attachment to Krishna and the Guru, the devotee keeps a strong association with other vaishnavas, in the form of 'satsang', or the act of communing together to discuss and deliberate upon Krishna lilas. Such association provides further enlightenment to each other and enriches the devotion of each vaishnava.

The great poets Surdas, Parmanandadas, Kumbhandas, and Krishnadas are the disciples of Shri Vallabhacharya. (For their vartas refer to the *Poetry* chapter)

The vaishnavas were very pious and spiritual in their thoughts and actions and they observed the principles of Pusti-Marg with great dedication. Shri Vallabhacharya initiated many more disciples in addition to these, but the '84 Vaishnavas' were the most important, and gave rise to the '84 Vaishnavas' stories. Below are examples of short episodes in the varta of four of the '84 Vaishnavas'. A full list of all '84 Vaishnavas' is also included below (names are in no particular order).

In certain places in this chapter, the term Mahaprabhuji is used instead of Vallabhacharya.

Shri Vallabhacharya's 84 Vaishnavas

1. Damodardas Harsani (Damala)
2. Krishnadas Meghan
3. Damordardas Sambhalavare and his maid
4. Padmanadas and his wife Parvati, daughter Tulsa and son Raghudas
5. Rajobai Chatrani
6. Seth Purshottamdas and his daughter, Rukhsmani
7. Ramdas Sarswat
8. Gadoadardas
9. Venidas and Madhavdas
10. Harivans Pathak
11. Govindas Bhalla
12. Amma Chatrani
13. Gadhandhavan Khatri
14. Narayandas Brahmachari
15. One Chatrani from Mahavan
16. Giyadas Shuri
17. Devakapur Khatri
18. Dinkardas Seth
19. Dinkardas and Mukundas
20. Prabhudas Jalota
21. Prabhudas Bhatt
22. Purshottamdas and his wife
23. Tripurdas Khayastha
24. Puranmal Khatri
25. Yadavendradas Kumbhar
26. Goisandas Sarsvat
27. Madhav Bhatt Kasmiri
28. Gopaldas from Vanvada
29. Padmaraval Sachora
30. Purshottamdas Joshi Sachora
31. Jagannath and Narahari Joshi and their mother
32. Rana Vyas Sachora
33. Ramdas Sachora
34. Govind Dube Sachora
35. Raja Dube and Madhav Dube
36. Uttanslokadas
37. Ishvardas Dube
38. Vasudevdas Chakda
39. Baba Venu, Krishnadas Gughri and Yadvandradas
40. Jagatananda from Thaneshwar
41. Ananddas Vishvambhardas
42. One Chatrani from Adel
43. One Chatrani from Prayag
44. Gorja and Sumari, wife and mother-in-law
45. Krishnadasi Khavasni
46. Bhulla Misra Sarsvat
47. Ramdas Mirabai na Purohit
48. Ramdas Chauhan
49. Ramananda Pandit
50. Vishnudas Chippa
51. Jivandas Khatri
52. Bhagwandas Sarsvat
53. Bhagwandas Sanchora
54. Achyutadas Sanodia
55. Achyutadas Gaura Brahmin
56. Achyutadas Sarsvat
57. Narayandas Kayastha
58. Narayandas Bhatt
59. Narayandas Lohana
60. One Chatrani from Sinhanand
61. Virbai, mother of Damodardas
62. Husband and wife from Sinhanand
63. One Suthar (Carpenter) from Adel
64. One Kshatriya from Purava
65. Laghu Purshottamdas
66. Kaviraj Bhatt from Mathura
67. Gopaldas from Indota
68. Janardandas Chopda
69. Garu Swami Sanodia
70. Kanaiyasal Khotri from Agra
71. Narharidas Godia Brahmin
72. Narhar Sanyasi
73. Sadhu Pande, Bhavani and Naro
74. Gopaldas Jathadhari
75. Krishnadas and his wife
76. Santdas Chopda
77. Sundardas and Madhodas
78. Mavaji Patel and his wife, Birajo
79. Gopaldas from Naroda
80. Bhadrayandas Brahmin
81. Surdas, Sarsvat Brahmin
82. Parmanandas Kanojiya Brahmin
83. Kumbhandasji Gorva Khatri
84. Krishnadas Adikari

Damodardas Harsani (Damala)

Damodardas was born at sunrise on Magh Sudh four of the Samvat year 1530 (AD 1473). At that very moment the entire area became filled with light, and many auspicious marks appeared on him.

Damodardas was never conscious of eating, sleeping, wearing his clothes or anything else except Shri Mahaprabhuji. When he was a child, he never took the slightest interest in anything worldly, passed his days sitting on the balcony, and waited for Mahaprabhuji's arrival. Damodardas grew ill and became a mere skeleton because of Mahaprabhuji's separation. His family members worried about him. After some days, Shri Mahaprabhuji came to Damodardas's town. Damodardas became very excited when he saw Mahaprabhuji and jumped right down from the balcony and grasped Shri Mahaprabhuji's feet. He suddenly received a new divine body that was filled with divine love for Shri Krishna.

Shri Mahaprabhuji lovingly called Damodardas by the name of Damala, which literally means, 'pure'. Damodardas's devotion to Shri Mahaprabhuji was only excelled by his devotion to the Lord Krishna.

Once, while Shri Mahaprabhuji was resting by the banks of the Yamuna river, he was thinking how he could fulfil the Lord's order to re-establish the relation of the people of this impure kali age with the divine God. Lord Krishna suddenly appeared in front of him and told him to uplift people through the "Brahma Sambhandh". Later, Shri Mahaprabhuji asked Damala, "Did you hear anything last night?" Damala replied, "I heard the Lord's voice, but I was not able to understand what he said".

Damala said he did not understand what the Lord had said and that if he had understood, then he would be on the same level as Shri Mahaprabhuji. For this reason, Damala had no real interest in hearing the Lord and was only concerned with becoming the devout disciple of Shri Mahaprabhuji. For the first time following the order of the Lord, Shri Mahaprabhuji gave "Brahma Sambhandh" to Damala and said: "Damala this path has been established for you".

On another occasion while in Jatipura at the Sunder Shilaji, Shri Mahaprabhuji was resting in Damala's lap when Shri Krishna appeared. Damala did not wake his beloved guruji. When Shri Mahaprabhuji awoke and saw the Lord standing a short distance away, and came to know the fact, he reprimanded Damala for his seemingly unjust action. The Lord interrupted and said, "Don't be angry with Damala, he is only keeping his dharma as your servant, and for him to have acted like this is certainly justified".

Shri Mahaprabhuji asked the Lord three times not to let Damala leave his body before him. The reason for this was that when Shri Mahaprabhuji would enter the sanyasa order of renunciates, his two sons Shri Gopinathji and Shri Gosainji would only be young boys and it would be necessary for someone to teach them the principles of the Pusti-Marg. For this work Damala was the perfect person. Shri Mahaprabhuji always read and discussed Shrimad Bhagvatam and other religious works in the presence of Damala and kept no secrets from him. Shri Mahaprabhuji firmly established in Damala's heart the Lord's lilas. Although Shri Mahaprabhuji had completed his mission, Damodardas continued giving true knowledge of his path to Shri Gosainji.

Once Shri Gosainji asked Damala, what he thought about Shri Mahaprabhuji. Damala replied that Shri Mahaprabhuji was even greater than the Lord. Shri Mahaprabhuji gives the priceless gift of Shri Nathji and for this reason is greater than the Lord.

Even as a disciple, Damodardas always told the stories of Shri Mahaprabhuji and gave advice to Shri Gosainji. Here we must understand that it was not actually Damala speaking but rather Shri Mahaprabhuji speaking through Damala. Even after Shri Mahaprahuji had left this world, he would give his divine sight to Damala every third day, because Damala's body could not bear any long time of separation from his blessed Guru, and would then enlighten Damala about Lord Krishna's intimate aspects. Shri Mahaprabhuji always lives in the heart of Damala, and he is the perfect example of a vaishnava.

Krishnadas Meghan

Before Krishnadas Meghan became a disciple of Shri Mahaprabhuji, he followed a yogi guru who told him that the Lord had been born upon Earth, but he was not sure of the location. Krishnadas was anxious to find the Lord, and decided to search for him. After many years he finally met Shri Mahaprabhuji, and recognising him to be an incarnation, he became his disciple and followed him wherever he went.

On one occasion when Shri Mahaprabhuji visited Shri Veda Vyasa, near Narayana in the Himalayas, they spent three days discussing one line from the Shrimad Bhagvatam. Veda Vyasa confessed that even he, the author of the Shrimad Bhagvatam, was not fully able to comprehend the depth of Shri Mahaprabhuji's explanation and could not therefore imbibe its entire nectar. For Shri Veda Vyasa, the incarnation of knowledge, only spoke the Bhagvatam but it was the Lord who actually composed it. The following poem by Harijivans conveys this point:

> *"To whom Krishna does not choose to reveal Himself, those people, even after reading and listening to all the Purana, Smritis and Vedas still don't know God. The creator, Brahma, heard the Shrimad Bhagavatam from Lord Narayana and then related it to the celestial sage, Narada. Narada passed on the great scripture to Shri Veda Vyasa who was not able to discover its true reality. For him, it was a medicine which removed his anxiety and pain. Veda Vyasa then taught the Bhagavata to Shri Shuka Deva who in turn recited it before King Parikshit. Even though the King heard the tenth canto, which depicts the Braja 'Lilas', he did not develop Total Love and consequently did not perform Krishna's 'seva'."*

> *"Shri Vallabh has churned the nectar curds of the Bhagavata to their perfection, and removing the veil of ignorance, bequeaths his devoted followers Shri Krishna. He reveals to them the varied nectars of Krishna's 'seva' and ornamentation. Says the poet Harijivan, by showering grace over divine souls, you let them taste divine flavour."*

On three occasions Krishnadas Meghan did such good deeds that Shri Mahaprabhuji asked him on each occasion to make a wish of his choice. On each of the three occasions Krishnadas Meghan asked (i) that the principles of Shri Mahaprabhuji's path remain firm in his heart (ii) that his speech be pure, and (iii) that Shri Mahaprabhuji visit his yogi guru's hermitage and make him Shri Mahaprabhuji's disciple. On each occasion Shri Mahaprabhuji granted him the first two wishes but refused to visit the yogi's hermitage. After some time Krishnadas Meghan asked Shri Mahaprabhuji if he could visit his yogi's hermitage, but Shri Mahaprabhuji replied that his trip would be disappointing, and indeed it was.

Arriving at the hermitage, his yogi guru immediately asked if he had made another guru. When Krishnadas Meghan said that he had found the Lord, his yogi guru doubted him. Krishnadas Meghan took some burning coal and said 'If Shri Mahaprabhuji is the Lord, my hands will not burn; otherwise let them burn to ashes'. His yogi guru grabbed his hands and made him drop the coals in his hands. Krishnasdas was distressed at his guru's disbelief and returned to Shri Mahaprabhuji's camp. Only after this incident did his devotion become single-minded, the path of devotion become established in his heart, and his speech become pure.

Once Krishnadas asked what Krishna enjoyed most, to which Mahaprabhuji replied that Krishna liked milk products, but was most fond of the love of his Bhaktas. On another occasion he asked what Krishna disliked, and Mahaprabhuji replied, confusion, strife, etc., and so these should be avoided. He also asked why some Vaishnavas did not realise Krishna's lila, and Mahaprabhuji explained that their surrender to the Lord was not perfect, they did not keep the association of accomplished vaishnavas, and lacked humility. He explained that one is able to realise Krishna through good association, constant contemplation of great devotional works, and the loving performance of Shri Krishna's seva.

Krishnadas's devotion to Shri Mahaprabhuji was so intense that when Mahaprabhuji left this world, he felt extreme separation from his guru, and left his body.

The Brothers: Jagannath and Narahari

Mrs Joshi became Shri Mahaprabhuji's disciple after her husband died for committing bad deeds, as had been predicted by Shri Mahaprabhuji. Shri Mahaprabhuji familiarised her with the moods and modes of *seva.* She had two children called Jagannath and Narahari. When they were a little older she asked them to visit Adel and become Shri Mahaprabhuji's disciples. She gave them a golden coin to offer to Shri Mahaprabhuji when they bowed to him, and explained that he was the Lord. Not fully believing their mother they set out for Adel, but discovered that Shri Mahaprabhuji was visiting Jagannath Puri. So they decided not to return home, and instead set out for Jagannath Puri.

When they arrived at Jagannath Puri, they met Shri Mahaprabhuji who immediately enquired 'Is your mother well?'. The boys were astonished that they had never met Shri Mahaprabhuji and yet he knew who they were. Shri Mahaprabhuji suggested that they visit the temple, and when they entered the temple they saw Shri Mahaprabhuji next to Lord Jagannath. They were perplexed, and thought that perhaps Shri Mahaprabhuji had come by another route. They went back and saw Shri Mahaprabhuji in the exact same spot where they had seen him before. Shri Mahaprabhuji enquired if they had seen Lord Jagannath, and asked 'Are your doubts removed?' The boys humbly said that before they had ignorantly doubted him, but that now they realised his divinity. Returning home to their mother they related the entire journey, and their mother questioned why they had doubted him when she had already explained that he was the Lord.

Narahari is humbled

On one occasion, during his journey to a place of pilgrimage where he could have sight of Shri Mahaprabhuji, Narahari prepared some bread and lentils at a camp near Patna. A beautiful boy came to him and asked for some food, which Narahari gave, and the boy then climbed a tree and disappeared. On the next day, again the boy came down from the tree and again asked for some food, but Narahari thought this was some kind of deception and did not give the boy anything. Krishna went to Jagannath, Narahari's brother, and narrated the entire episode to him. On the following day Jagannath asked his brother who was the boy who came for food. Hearing his brother he realised that he had made a terrible mistake and that the boy was actually the Lord himself, and he questioned how as a disciple of Shri Mahaprabhuji he could have been so deceived. Narahari was humbled by this experience, his heart was purified by intense feelings of devotion and he too experienced Krishna.

Jagannath offers Hot Pudding

On one occasion when Shri Mahaprabhuji visited Jagannath, Krishna complained to him that he had burnt his tongue and hand whilst trying to eat the boiling rice pudding that Jagannath had given him. When Shri Mahaprabhuji asked Jagannath why he had offered hot rice pudding to Krishna, he answered that he thought it was to be offered hot, but Shri Mahaprabhuji explained to him that this was not in fact the case.

Henceforth Jagannath no longer offered hot rice pudding to Krishna.

A Rajput tries to kill Jagannath

Some confusion once occurred when, at a temple, an elderly lady threw a garland at the Lord. Jagannath picked it up and threw it outside because it was prohibited to throw garlands at the Lord, but it landed on one of the Rajputs. However, another Rajput thought that the honour of receiving the garland should be his and so decided to kill Jagannath! At an opportune moment the Rajput attempted to kill Jagannath with a sword from behind, but at that very moment Krishna appeared, grabbed his hand, and asked him not to kill Jagannath. The Rajput then realised that Jagannath was an enlightened soul and fell to his feet and prayed, begging for his mercy. Jagannath took the Rajput to his home, and asked him to repeat Krishna's sacred names. This is an example of how devotees like Jagannath are so imbued with faith that they can liberate even those harbouring ill feeling towards them.

Why Shri Mahaprabhuji's Disciples are thin

In another varta, there is described an incident in which Shri Mahaprabhuji was asked by Sanatan Goswami, a disciple of Shri Krishna Chaitanya, why the path was called Pusti-Marg (Pusti means grace "of nourishment") yet all the disciples who followed the path were all thin. Shri Mahaprabhuji explained that he had warned the disciples 'not to enter into this path, but not heeding my sound advice, they are suffering the consequences'. Sanatan Gosvami, unable to grasp the true meaning of Shri Mahaprabhuji's reply, returned to Jagannath Puri, and relayed the conversation to his guru, Shri Krishna Chaitanya. Upon hearing this Shri Krishna Chaitanya fell unconscious into a trance. The Gosvami relayed the incident three times to his guru and each time Shri Krishna Chaitanya fell into a trance contemplating the transcendental essence of Shri Mahaprabhuji 's response.

Just as Krishna had requested the Gopis return to their homes and husbands, and they disregarded Him, forgetting their physical needs in His presence, and instead gathered to listen to His sweet flute and taste the fruits of His presence; in the same way Shri Mahaprabhuji discouraged the bhaktas from entering the path, Pusti-Marg, but they too disregarded Him and forgot their physical requirements in their desire to experience the Path of Grace.

Varta of 252 Vaishnavas

Shri Gosainji, son of Shri Vallabhacharya handed down the vartas of the '252 Vaishnavas' to Shri Gokulnathji, grandson of Shri Vallabhacharya. Shri Gokulnathji recited them in the presence of his disciples who included the great poets of Asta-Chaap, namely Nanandas, Govinda Svami, Chita Svami and Chatrabhujdas. The vartas of these disciples are described in the *Poetry* chapter.

The '252 Vaishnavas', or disciples, are all part of Shri Vitthalnathji's divine form, and are made up of three groups of 84 which are predominantly *tamasik, rajasik, and sattvic.*

Again, Shri Hariraiji's Bhava Prakash provides a deeper understanding of the lives of the vaishnavas.

Chapter Six

Poetry

Asta-Chaap, eight devotional poets and Dayaram

As vaishnava Shyamdas describes in his writings, the Asta-Chaap poets composed some of the finest poetry written in the Braja Bhasya language. Of course, there are many other fine Krishna poets of the era such as Hit Harivams, Svami Haridas, Shri Bhatt, Mirabai, but these eight devotional poets sang before Shri Nathji on the Govardhan Hill and were the intimate friends of Lord Krishna who actually experienced his "lila" firsthand.

Surdas, Parmanandadas, Kumbhandas and Krishnadas form part of the '84 Vaishnavas' stories, and Nanandas, Govinda Svami, Chita Svami and Chatrabhujdas form part of the '252 Vaishnavas' stories, the former received initiation by Shri Vallabhacharya (Shri Mahaprabhuji), the latter by his son Shri Vitthalnathji (Shri Gosainji). Between them, being only a generation apart, they composed a wealth of unprecedented devotional works. All the poets lived and composed their works in the period between AD 1479 and approximately 1600.

These poets actually played with and talked to Krishna, who showed them his "sakha bhava". Therefore each poet expresses aspects of his uniquely intimate relationship with Shri Krishna in his poetry.

The following extracts therefore exemplify the "pusti" highlighting the mainly child-like lilas that the Asta-Chaap poets themselves witnessed. All eight poets convey a deep feeling of humility and, completely unlike ideas from their imagination, or

"Kalpana", the poets' expressions and descriptions are spontaneous feelings at having seen Krishna's lilas with their own eyes. This is an important distinction. The poetry expresses their devotional experiences, not their imagined experiences.

The poetry in this section is a reproduction of the English translation by Shyamdas [reference 42].

Surdas

Surdas is arguably the best known of the poets. He was born in 1479, a disabled child with no eyes or eyesockets, only eyebrows. His Sarasvata Brahman parents cared little for Surdas and did not know what to do with him; they were a very poor family, and Surdas' disability was a strain. But Surdas had an inner strength and an amazing gift of sight in his mind's eye. He could meditate and see the whereabouts of things that had gone missing.

One day, when his father was distraught at the loss of two gold coins that would feed the family for the next two months, Surdas made a deal with his father, that if he could locate the coins, his father would allow Surdas to leave. His father agreed, Surdas disclosed the location of the coins, and at the age of only six, left his family home in Sihin, eight miles from Delhi, and went to live by the edge of a lake, where he resided for the next eighteen years.

News of Surdas' ability spread and people came to him for help to locate what they had lost. Notably, Surdas assisted a rich farmer to find his lost sheep, and from that day on, the farmer ensured that Surdas never wanted for food or shelter.

One night however, Surdas came to realise that to meet the Lord he had to renounce his home, his personal glory and the material gains it afforded him, and instead to use his life for the glory of the Lord. The next morning he left his home by the lake, and went to Go Ghat on the holy banks of the Yamuna river. Here in 1511 he met Shri Mahaprabhuji.

When Surdas had bathed in the Yamuna river, Shri Mahaprabhuji gave him an "ashtakshara mantra" and then initiated him with "Brahma Sambhandh". Through the "ashtakshara mantra" all of his sins were absolved and he received the seven devotional practices: to hear the Lord's praises, to chant them, to remember them, to wait upon Him, to offer worship and salutations to Him, and to dedicate his actions to Him. After receiving "Brahma Sambhandh", Surdas achieved the last two states of the nine-fold devotion, and then received the highest devotional lila when Shri Mahaprabhuji explained to him the content of the tenth canto of Bhagvatam. On hearing this Surdas had a complete grasp of Shri Mahaprabhuji's entire Shri Subodhini.

Through Mahaprabhuji's grace, Surdas began to experience all of Shri Krishna's lilas while sitting on the banks of the Yamuna river. He also sang a long poem about the birth of Shri Krishna. He was always humble and considered himself a simple, poor soul.

Through experiencing the predominately child lila of Krishna, Surdas experienced feelings of tenderness and a lightness of the divine relationship, which he captures and reflects in many of his poems.

> Krishna has a little face
> and little feet,
> and on his little hand
> there is a little butter.
> He has little lips,
> and with his little laugh
> he steals everyone's heart.
>
> Little cheeks
> a little brow
> and wears little clothes
> and little ornaments.
>
> Sur prays,
> to a little crowing Krishna:
> "Shower a little grace
> and shelter me."

Krishna can be little, steal butter or clothes from the Gopis, and can still remain divine. Krishna can perfectly maintain all contradictions. Surdas' devotion is filled with such child-like divine acts of play. Surdas also displays a deep commitment to his guru Shri Vallabhacharya, who opened his eyes to Krishna lilas, as exemplified by the following poem:

> In his sacred feet,
> have your faith's firm seat.
>
> Moonbeams shine from
> the nails of Vallabh's feet.
>
> Without their light,
> the worlds in blindness stray.
>
> Impossible in Kali's day
> to find the final way.
>
> In two ways blind,
> a wageless servant Sur does say.

Once when Chatrabhujdas questioned why Surdas, being a great poet, had composed over one hundred thousand poems, but had never sung the glories of Shri Mahaprabhuji, Surdas responded with the above poem illustrating that he never saw any difference between Shri Mahaprabhuji and Lord Krishna.

In the poem Surdas reveals his heart. He explains that devotees should have firm faith in Shri Mahaprabhuji's feet. Without the brilliance which shines from his toenails, the entire world remains engulfed in darkness. The only way to overcome the Kali age of struggle is to take refuge in Shri Mahaprabhuji.

Parmanandadas

Parmanandadas means "supreme bliss", and the name was given to him by his Brahmin parents because firstly, they felt blessed by the Lord to have been given a son, and secondly, on the day of his birth in Kanoja, his parents were given a large sum of money by a rich man.

Parmanandadas had a happy childhood, and grew to be a great poet with a vast following. He composed a wealth of poetry. One time he went to Prayag for the Maha Makar bath festivals, but he stayed there for many years and sang every night by the edge of the lake. Knowing he had miraculous powers, people would come to him with their problems. Parmanandadas would sing for several hours, but on the eleventh lunar day he sang all through the night stopping before sunrise. Whilst resting afterwards, he dreamt that child Krishna was sitting on Kapurs lap, a disciple of Shri Mahaprabhuji, and had been listening to him. On the next day he felt the scintillating beauty of Shri Krishna's form, and felt the urge to meet Mahaprabhuji. He set out across the river to Adel, where Shri Mahaprabhuji was residing. Shri Mahaprabhuji initiated him and explained to him the tenth canto of the Shrimad Bhagvatam, when he began to experience the Lord's form and all of his lilas. Then Parmanandadas sang songs of Krishna's child lila throughout the day for Navanita Priyaji.

O friend,
the beautiful lotus-eyed Shyam
swings in the cradle.
All the Braja maidens sing his child 'lilas'.

The jewel-like nails
of Krishna's red tender lotus feet
are brilliant like the sun.

His curly locks
are like lines of black bees.
A necklace strung with large pearls
swings on his neck.

Krishna grabs his toe with his lotus hand
and puts it in his mouth.

Seeing his reflection,
he laughs and laughs.

Queen Yashoda looks at her heap of fortune,
her darling son.

Parmanandadas Svami nourishes
love for young Gopal.

Then he sang:

> "Yashoda, your fortune is beyond description
> That form which Brahma and other gods
> have difficulty realizing
> has now appeared for you.
>
> Shiva, Narada, and Sanaka and other great sages
> try to find a way to meet Him.
>
> The same Lord, Nanda's son,
> covered with dust,
> wraps his hands around your neck."
>
> She sees Krishna's smiling face
> as he rests in the jewelled cradle
> and says,
> "Swing my son, I'll celebrate."
> Paramanandadas celebrates

Shri Mahaprabhuji had many disciples but only Parmanandadas and Surdas were such highly prolific poets.

Kumbhandas

Kumbhandas met Shri Mahaprabhuji at the Govardhan Hill and Shri Mahaprabhuji gave him the task of singing every day for Shri Nathji. Shri Nathji would appear before the poet often playing and talking to him. They had a mutual love and Khumbandas could not bear to be separated from Shri Nathji.

On one occasion Kumbhandas sang before Shri Nathji:

> My eyes don't even blink
> when I see that form
> Beholding Krishna
> my eyes and heart
> stick to his every part.
> How to describe.
> I can't utter a word.

The one who begs for curds
has taken off with my mind.
Sings Kumbhandas,
"When Krishna encounters the Gopis
he tells them beautiful things."

* * * * *

Friend, he has become the door guards to these eyes
Friend, how to stop those Khanjan[1] eyes?
When he comes down the path,
I can't close my lids

Friend, I am flooded with love
and spy by day and by night
upon his every pleasure

Friend, for Kumbhanadas's Lord
Govardhandhar,
these eyes are searching

Shri Mahaprabhuji taught Khumbandas and explained to him the principles of the Path of Grace. Khumbandas spent his whole life singing only for Shri Nathji. He would never sing for other people and even refused monarchs. One day, after Shri Nathji's seva, the weary Khumbandas sat beside the Sankarshana lake just below Shri Nathji's temple, and told his son Chatrbhujdas, "in an hour or so I will leave this body". He sang a final poem for Shri Gosainji, then left his body and entered the Lord's lila.

Krishnadas

When Krishnadas was born in Chilotara, Gujarat into a "sudra" family, his father, the ruler of the town, asked local Brahmin sages to predict Krishnadas' life. They told him his son would be a great "bhakta", that he would leave the family home, and that he should be named "Krishnadas".

Sure enough, Krishnadas did indeed leave the family home, after a bitter dispute with his father. Krishnadas went to Matharu and to the Govardhan Hill where he knew that a temple to Shri Nathji had been constructed. From the moment Krishnadas saw him, his heart belonged to

(1) Khanjan birds are known for their lovely eyes.

Shri Nathji, who in turn told Shri Mahaprabhuji, that at last, after a long separation, Krishnadas had finally arrived. Shri Mahaprabhuji initiated Krishnadas, who was then appointed manager of the temple, and Krishnadas began to experience all of the Lord's lilas.

Once, Shri Nathji told Krishnadas to go with the drummer Shyam Kumar to the Chandra lake in Parasoli, where he would perform the "Rasalila". And there, Krishna and the Gopis danced in a most dazzling way whilst Krishnadas sang and Shyam Kumar played many songs.

One day Surdas and Krishnadas got into a dispute. Surdas accused Krishnadas of copying all his poems, telling him to write one of his own efforts. For hours Krishnadas struggled to come up with an original work that bore no resemblance to anything Surdas had written. Fruitless, he went off to eat, and whilst away, Shri Nathji wrote the following poem:

> With his cowherds, Krishna comes from
> the forest.
>
> His curly locks are covered with the dust of the
> 'Nachuki' cows.
>
> His brow is bowed like the
> love god's
> His sidelong glances are
> the arrows.
>
> His head is embellished with a delightful crown.
> His splendid face appears as the moon.
>
> Gazing upon it,
> fresh lotus like women become frenzied.
> His closed lips are like the bimba fruit.
> When he grins, his teeth appear
> like rows of jasmine flowers.
>
> Earrings on his ears,
> a ring in his nose,
> a tilak in his brow;

the Kostubhamani jewel around his neck
matched with three other fine necklaces.
Another golden jewel-inlaid necklace
hangs by a pendant on his chest.

Within that necklace shines a white string of pearls.
On his wrist, bangles,
on his long arms, armlets,
rings on his finger.
His fingernails are jewelled.

The sound of his flute
enchants the entire world
and ties the Gopis' heart
in the knot of love.

His belled waist sash
embedded with diamonds.
The lines around his lotus navel
like rows of black bees.

Sometimes he runs and skips for his bhaktas'
benefit.

Beloved Krishna's cheeks are beautified
with strings of sweat beads.

His gracious form is draped in a yellow cloth.
His ankles ring out with his gait.

The Holder of the Mountain resides
in Krishnadas's heart.
The brilliance of his toenails
destroys the darkness.

Chatrabhujdas

In 1540, Kumbhandas's sixth son was born into the Kshatriya caste in Yamunavata. He gave him the name "Chatrabhujdas", meaning "servant of the four-armed Lord", after a recent adventure he had shared with Shri Nathji. One day, whilst playing together, they went to steal cur and butter. When the Lord grasped a jug of curd, his shawl fell to the ground.

With his hands already full, two more arms appeared from his body and scooped up the shawl. Kumbhandas had witnessed Krishna's chatrabhuja, his four-armed form. Kumbhandas brought his child to Shri Gosainji for initiation before Shri Nathji. And after receiving the sacred mantra, Chatrabhujdas could experience Krishna's lilas. Both Kumbhandas and Chatrabhujdas were Krishna's best friends and through his grace were great bhaktas, and given the direct experience of his presence.

On one occasion of Shri Mahaprabhuji's birthday, Shri Gosainji made special offerings and ornamentation to Krishna, upon which Chatrabhujdas sang:

> Spying Krishna's elaborate ornamentation
> she takes mirror in hand
> to show her beloved saying,
> "At one glimpse of you I rejoice
> Today your splendour is beyond words.
>
> On each part of your body
> exquisite clothes and jewels.
> Resplendent, you enchant my mind."
>
> The Braja maiden thrills in every pore
> and makes a fragrant flower garland.
>
> She waves her shawl around her love
> in celebration.
>
> The wishes of her mind and body bounding.
> Chatrabhujdas drinks the nectar of Krishna's form.

A vaishnava asked Shri Gosainji what was so special about this day such that Chatrabhujdas had sung, "Today your splendour is beyond words". Shri Gosainji suggested that he ask Chatrabhujdas, who in response sang:

> Friend, today, tomorrow, yes, everyday,
> behold the nectar-filled Holder of the Mountain
>
> What poet can possibly illustrate
> his clothes and ornaments?

Every moment his beauty is fresh again,
his every part, an ocean of graciousness,
more spellbinding than a billion love gods.

His beauty upsurges waves
and captures the heart of the world.

Chatrabhujdas imbibes Shri Nathji's sweet form
and lives forever in his shelter.

The vaishnava was still unable to fathom the essence, and subsequently Shri Gosainji explained, "Today, Shri Mahaprabhuji's appearance day, Shri Svaminiji prepared all the offerings and ornamentations with her own hands, thus pleasing Shri Nathji. So, Chatrabhujdas sang, "Today your splendour is beyond words". He sang a second poem by the Govinda lake, in which he explained the actions of the Braja women who constantly offered food and gifts to Krishna, who in turn accepted them lovingly and fulfilled their desires. Therefore, "Shri Nathji is splendorous every moment".

Chatrabhujdas's guru, Shri Gosainji entered a cave on the Govardhan Hill and left this world. His sons and disciples experienced great grief. When Chatrabhujdas who was at home, heard the news, he ran to the cave and fell to his knees in tears. Shri Gosainji, knowing that Chatrabhujdas suffered greatly from the separation, appeared to him in his divine form and consoled him saying, " I am always near you". Then Chatrabhujdas sang the glories of his guru, setting his heart upon his lotus feet, and left his body, entering into the Lord's lila. His son Raghodas and all the vaishnavas completed Chatrabhujdas's last rites.

Chita Svami

Little is known of Chita Svami's early life. He was a Chaube Brahmin, believed to have been born around 1516 in Mathura, and he led a group of four other Brahmins of questionable nature. He was known as Chitu.

One day all five agreed to attempt to deceive Shri Gosainji by giving him a false offering of an empty coconut and a counterfeit coin. Arriving in Gokul, Chita Svami went in first to see Shri Gosainji. When he looked upon Shri Gosainji he was amazed to see Krishna, and immediately he repented his deception and implored to be accepted as the Lord's disciple. Asking what offering Chita Svami had brought, Shri Gosainji had one of his helpers cut open the empty coconut in front of Chita Svami who was amazed to see a ripe fruit cut in half.

Soon afterwards Shri Gosainji initiated Chita Svami before Shri Navanita Priyaji, and from that day forwards Chita Svami's great renown started to grow because of the many poems that he composed.

On one occasion Chita Svami sang the following poem on the divine nature of his guru's seven sons:

> Krishna takes on the seven forms
> of Shri Gosainji's son
> and plays.
>
> Shri Vitthalnath forever appears
> in the clan of Brahmins,
> blessing us with 'bhakti.'
>
> Shri Girdhar, king of kings,
> has arisen to dwell in Braja.
>
> Shri Govinda is a moon
> who peruses the world with nectar beams.
>
> Shri Bal Krishna has wide eyes
> his beauty abashes billions of love gods.
> Shri Gokulnathji is filled with splendid qualities,
> a treasure of compassion and mercy.
>
> Those who have accumulated pious merit
> take the shelter of Shri Raghunath,
> Shri Yadunath, and Shri Ghanshyam.
>
> Says Chita Svami, "Shri Vitthal is Krishna.
> By worshipping Him, all is transcended.
> From eldest to youngest." [1]

(1) Chita Svami signs most of his poems in this way, since his devotion to his guru and to God were inseparable.

Nanandas

The younger brother of the great Tulsidas (the famous saint-devotee who wrote the Ramcharitramanis in praise of Lord Rama), Nanandas was born in Rampura in the northeast of India. He had a great love of life, and unlike his devout brother, would idle away his time watching dance shows. When a group of people passed through the town on their way to Gujurat's sacred Dwarkanathji, Nanandas was motivated to join them, and set off despite his brother's dire warnings that the journey would be beset with problems.

When the group then chose to spend a few days at Mathura village en route, Nanandas decided to continue on alone, and was soon heading in the wrong direction towards Punjab. His error had lead him to the hometown of a Kshatriya and into trouble, for when Nanandas saw the face of the Kshatriya's wife, he was completely mesmerised, seeing Lord Krishna within it, and began to call upon the Kshatriya's wife daily, until the gossiping and speculation in the town forced the Kshatriya to move his family to Gokul.

Even their migration did not deter the mesmerised Nanandas who followed them to the shores of the Yamuna river, where he sat and sang odes of love to Yamuna. Only the words of his songs revealed how he had confused the face of the Kshatriya's wife for that of Krishna's, and his deep love for Krishna. The Kshatriya paid the boatmen not to ferry Nanandas across the river and took his family to their guru Shri Gosainji and explained the events that had brought them to Gokul. Of course, the omniscient Shri Gosainji already understood everything. He consoled them saying that their intervention had brought the great bhakta Nanandas to him, and that now Nanandas would trouble them no more.

Shri Gosainji sent for Nanandas, and when he saw the Lord's face, his mind was instantly cleared of any confusion. Shri Gosainji took Nanandas as his disciple and through his grace, showed him Shri Navanita Priyaji and Shri Nathji, and Nanandas sang:

> Krishna comes from the forest
> with his friends
> behind the cows.

The beauty of the dust on his curly locks
charms; indescribable splendour.

The jingling bells on his dazzling sash
allure.

He wanders about,
playing sweet melodious tunes on his flute.

Yashoda wipes the face
of Nanandas' Lord
and kisses him without fatigue.

* * * * *

The women of Gokul make excuses
to come to Yashoda's home.

Not seeing Krishna's great face
time won't pass.

Once they see that countenance,
they forget their household work.

They borrow a light from Yashoda's house
and on the way home extinguish it.

Returning once again,
they elaborately blame the wind.

Nanandas' eyes are stuck to Nanda's son.
Without seeing him
a moment passes like four eons.

* * * * *

Nanandas lived for six months with Surdas near the Govardhan Hill at Parasoli, and sang many such poems for Shri Nathji.

Govinda Svami (Govindadas)

Born around 1505, Govinda Svami lived in Antari, a town near the Govardhan Hill. He was a great and prolific poet.

When, one day, Govinda Svami learnt that it was possible to know Krishna's lila through Shri Gosainji, he immediately went to Gokul to meet him. He soon after became his disciple and renounced life with his own family, instead residing in Gokul from where he would frequently go to Mahavan, and receive sight of Krishna whilst singing. Govindadas always refused to bathe in the Yamuna river, believing her to be the sacred consort of Krishna, and as such, too beautiful and holy for his own worthless, unsacred body.

Together with Kumbhandas, Govindadas was an intimate friend of Shri Nathji and Shri Gosainji showed them everything of Krishna. Sometimes Shri Nathji and Govindadas would even play alone at the far side of the Govardhan Hill.

On one spring evening Shri Govindadas spontaneously sang the following, while witnessing Shri Gosainji offering a betal leaf to Shri Nathji:

> Govardhan Lal, eyes wide and shifting,
> your breast is decked
> with a forest garland.
> You enchant all the women of Braja.
>
> Frolicking playfully,
> Krishna arrives on the path
> where the ladies go to fetch water.
>
> He tugs the jugs off their heads;
> no one is allowed to draw from the well.
> The son of Nanda romps and fills the hearts
> of all the Gopis when they behold his face.
>
> Beloved Krishna covers his hands
> with a paste of vermilion powder.
>
> He stealthily sneaks up,
> smears the Gopis cheeks,
> and dashes away.

At this point Shri Gosainji questioned, "Why don't you finish the song?"

"Maharaja," Govindadas replied, "my mind is entangled in Him and, as I have sung, he dashed away. Now, how can there be more song when Krishna has left?"

Fascinated by this response, later that evening Shri Gosainji descended the hill, and completed Govindadas'poem.

> In this way Krishna plays
> the spring sport of 'Holi' with the Braja damsels.
> Over Govardhan's form
> Govinda's people rejoice.

This poetry reveals two important points as Shyamdas explains:

Firstly, Shri Gosainji signed the poem 'Jana Govinda', translated as 'Govinda's people' those who will never take birth again.

Secondly, Shri Govindadas, as well as other poets, experienced the lila firsthand with their own eyes, and sponteaneously described it in their verses. Once Shri Nathji disappeared, Govindadas could no longer witness the lila, and so concluded the poem, because the inspiration for his verse had departed.

When Shri Gosainji was about to leave his body, he took Govindadas by the arm and together they walked into a cave on the Govardhan Hill. And in that spot by the Sunder Shilaji in Jatipura, Shri Gosainji rejoined Krishna's eternal lila.

Dayaram [(*)]

Dayaram (AD 1777-1852) was one of the greatest poets in the Gujarati language. He was one of the most sectarian poets of medieval Gujarat - in contrast to other poets such as Narisimha, Miram and Dhiro who remained non-sectarian. Dayaram was a firm believer in and follower of Shri Vallabhacharya's Suddhadvaita philosophy and Pusti-Marg, receiving Brahma Sambhandh from Goswami Vallabhlalji. Much of his poetry was influenced by the Pusti-Marg traditions and it is because of this as well as the fact that some 250 years (over a quarter of a millennium) after Shri Vallabhacharya's time a poet was still expressing his poems and lyrics in the same devotional subject, that a small section

(*) Material taken from Dwyer, R. [reference 12] and Shyamdas [reference 45].

of his works is included here, alongside the great Asta-Chaap poets.

Dayaram knew very well the sixteen works of Shri Vallabhacharya's Shodas Grantha (see page 64, in the *Writings* chapter.) and they were the inspiration for his own philosophical poetry. Throughout Dayaram's poems devotion to Krishna and an understanding of Shri Vallabhacharya's teachings can be seen.

As the following extracts of poetry and comments have been taken from Pusti Asmita, spellings may vary from elsewhere in this book.

Dayaram sings:

> Give this servant your devotion.
> Mountain holders, holder of virtues
> O Lord, remove my grief,
> Shower love upon me.
>
> Supreme performer, son of Nanda,
> I love your enchanting form,
> My mind adheres to nothing else,
> Not even to the peerless omnipresent Brahman.
>
> I don't recite "I am Brahman"
> Nor do I like to hear the soundless sound
> I have no taste for sacrifice
> Or for the meditation of samadhi.
>
> I have no taste for heaven or liberation.
> I don't like spiritual drills devoid of Gopal.
> They are tasteless.
> I only savor the honor of his love.
>
> I adore my guru, Vallabh's son
> He is similar to my Krishna.
> Souls can not see God through any rehearsal.
> It happens only when My beloved awards it.
>
> I have searched but have found no essence.
> The only delight I know is in
> His seva and remembrance.
> On behalf of Shri Mahaprabhu, bless me Lord of Radha.

Dispel my ignorance at its root.
In the Vrindavan glades
Where you rendezvous with Radha
There, take hold of my hand Hari.

* * * * *

Shyamdas goes on to explain, “In the following short extract from Dayaram’s poem Shyam Manohar provides his commentary, and also by way of an example of the river and the ocean, explains forms of Brahman and the place of Pusti Bhakti.”

Krishna is euphoric and
Sports in the realm of devotion
That is free of hypocrisy.

He graces those who belong to
The Path of Grace and are Vallabh’s people.
Krishna, you are beloved of life itself.

Now place my mind at your lotus feet.
You fulfill all desires.
Now everyone, sing and dance.

“The Path of Grace means the Path of Devotion. The ability for the soul to enter the Path of Devotion is all attained through the grace of the “paramatma”, Shri Krishna. The blessed soul is not interested in worldly pursuits like wealth, position, fame or recognition. Devotion is never used to achieve the pleasure of such trivial pursuits. If you use devotion for worldly gain, that style of devotion could never be called Pusti or grace-filled. The heights of pusti bhakti can never be approached by devotion that either generates fear or a sense of false renunciation. Those who are either “too worldly attached” or “too worldly renounced” cannot grasp the true meaning of pusti.”

“From the grace-filled ocean of the Super Soul arises a cloud. Its downpour is comprised of its essence. The world can pull you away from that essence, yet sometimes the jiva can flow in the pure river of grace that is created from the downpours of that cloud. The river of grace that is created from the downpour of that cloud is what we call Pusti Bhakti. That river overcomes the ups and downs of the land while it is on its continuous flow towards the ocean and in that state its waters are called a river. A body of water that does not have any limitations or single direction of flow, is content within its self and creates waves and is also unobstructed is called an ocean. Both are essentially water but if viewed from the angle of form, they certainly appear to be different. Understand the difference and similarities between the river and the ocean and see how Brahman is playing with Brahman."

The following composition is an extract from Dayaram's *Bhaktiposana*, 'The nourishment of bhakti', consisting of 101 candravala verses originally written in Braj.

First I bow my guru, Shri Mahaprabhuji,
To Shri Vitthalnathji, Shri Krishna and to Shri Yamuna.
They are exalted and fulfill all desires.
The bhakta Damodardas also accomplishes my aspirations.
Let the eight Astha Chhap poets live within my heart.
Give me an auspicious mind unspoiled
That will nourish my devotion
And enable me to sing of your virtues.
Serve Shri Krishna, the graceful one.

The four Vedas and holy scriptures repeatedly contemplate.
The Upanisadas also probe for the meaning
And have come up with this nectar;
The essence is Krishna bhakti.
Have attachment to sat sang
As well as to Hari's feet.
They are invincible,
Take their refuge.
Serve Shri Krishna, the graceful one.

None are equal to him.
There is no lord above him.
Everything arise from him.
He is the master of all.
All divinities bow before him.
The Vedas try to describe him
And say, "Not that, not that."

He is not attained by
Shesh, Mahesh, Brahma or Laxshsmi.
He is called the Complete One.
Serve Shri Krishna, the graceful one.

In following Krishna there is joy
And not in merging with the Lord of the world.
The satisfaction of that seer is like the one
Who cuts his head off in hopes of obtaining a turban.
Now there is no place for his turban.
O Foolish one,
You haven't carefully considered your plan.
Water can not taste water.
Only if you remain separate can you taste him,
Serve Shri Krishna, the graceful one.

The attributes of love are:
Desire in the eyes
Remembrance, longing, and anxiety.
The three stages of attachment are
Sickness, weeping and madness.
Addiction then follows with
Unconsciousness and fainting.
When you are totally absorbed

Amongst his composition *Rasikavallabha*, 'The beloved of connoisseurs' (1838), consisting of 109 verses, is considered the most important. Written in Gujarati in a form of a dialogue between a teacher and his pupil, it expounds the major doctrines of the Pusti-Marg, namely, the nature *of brahma, jiva, jagat,* and the importance of *bhakti*. (See Sandesara, B.J. [reference 34]). Dayaram also composed Pustipatharahasya, 'The secret of the Pustimarga', consisting of 183 duha and rasavala verses in Gujarati, expressing devotion to the sect and particularly to its founders, their descendents and the vaishnav bhaktas. For further details on this and other philosophical works relating to the sect refer to a recent text by Rachel Dwyer (2001), on The Poetics of Devotion.

Chapter Seven

The 84 Bethaks

Pilgrimage sites of Shri Vallabhacharya

The 84 bethaks, are some of the principal locations visited by Shri Vallabhacharya in the course of his three pilgrimages across India. His main aim and intention was to spread religious knowledge and enlighten others to Krishna lila and he recited the Shrimad Bhagvatam in the majority of these 84 locations, which have themselves become pilgrimage sites for Shri Vallabhacharya's followers.

During his pilgrimages, or Bharat–yatras, Shri Vallabhacharya kept three observations: (a) not to wear any footwear, (b) not to wear any stitched clothing, merely dhoti and uperna, and (c) where possible, to camp outside the city and village boundaries, under a tree in a serene locale, usually near a river or a fresh-water pond. His pilgrimage started from Kashi (no 27) in Uttar Pradesh, (see the map on page 58), and first reached Chitrakut (no 24), before continuing onwards to his birthplace in Champaranya (no 32) in Madhya Pradesh, where he recited Shrimad Bhagvatam, uniquely revealing the Vedic knowledge in a disclosure spanning seven days. The bethaks can be visited anywhere from Shri Mudrachal (no 82) in Himachal Pradesh, to Rameshvar (no 41) in Tamil Nadu and from Dwarka (no 60) in Gujurat, to Jagannath Puri (no 34) in Orissa. However a large number of bethaks can be found in the Vraj in Uttar Pradesh and in the state of Gujurat. Followers believe that Shri Vallabhacharya still lives in his supernatural form at each of the 84 bethaks.

The bethaks are revered in three divine forms, the materialistic form - Adhibhautik, the spiritual form - Adhyatmika, and transcendental form - Adhidaivika. The physical structure of the bethak seen by the eye is the material form, the events that took place in the bethak or the divine pastimes of Shri Vallabhacharya is the spiritual form, and the continuing presence of Shri Vallabhacharya in all the bethaks is the trasendental form. The Adhibhautik form can be seen by all, but the latter two forms can be experienced only through the divine grace of the lord.

It was Shri Gokulnathji (AD 1551 - 1640), the fourth son of Shri Gosainji, and grandson of Shri Vallabhacharya, who revealed the bethaks to the entire world through his daily satsang with his intimate disciples. The compilation of his teaching became known as *Baithak Charitra*.

Today, the number of visitors has increased immensely, and many of the bethaks are now marked with temples, where daily tribute is paid to Shri Vallabhacharya and his religious teachings. Visiting the bethaks remain a lifelong aim and fascination for many of the followers. The quiet, serene, and calm environment together with disclosures on the Vallabh Siddhant evoke divine vibrations and happiness in thousands of followers who visit the bethaks, from all walks of life and from all over the world, throughout the year.

Followers make diligent preparations for visiting the bethaks, choosing with care the correct clothing to wear and offerings to be made, even fasting for 24 hours prior to the visit. Once at the bethak site, the follower observes a ritual of cleansing the body (aparasa), then dressing in the clean clothing, before making the offerings at Shri Vallabhacharya's shrine whilst reciting prayers and extracts from Shri Vallabhacharya's writings, as well as solemnly reflecting upon his life and teachings.

A map indicating a selection of the 84 bethaks, which clearly illustrates the geographical scope of the pilgrimages, can be found following the full list of bethaks on the next page.

Shri Vallabhacharya's 84 Bethaks

1. Govind Ghat, Gokul – Uttar Pradesh
2. Shri Bade Bethakji, Gokul – Uttar Pradesh
3. Shri Dwarkanathji's Temple, Gokul – Uttar Pradesh
4. Bansibat Na Bathekji, Vrindavan – Uttar Pradesh
5. Shri Vishranti Ghat, Mathura – Uttar Pradesh
6. Shri Madhuvan Na Bethakji, Mathura – Uttar Pradesh
7. Kamodvran, Mathura – Uttar Pradesh
8. Bahulavan, Mathura – Uttar Pradesh
9. Radha Kund, Mathura – Uttar Pradesh
10. Mansi Ganga, Mathura – Uttar Pradesh
11. Parasoli (Shri Chandra Sarovar), Mathura – Uttar Pradesh
12. Anyor, Mathura – Uttar Pradesh
13. Shri Govind Kund, Mathura – Uttar Pradesh
14. Shri Sundar Shila, Mathura – Uttar Pradesh
15. Giriraj Mountain, Mathura – Uttar Pradesh
16. Kamavan, Bharatpur – Rajasthan
17. Gahavaran, Barsana Mathura – Uttar Pradesh
18. Sanket, Mathura – Uttar Pradesh
19. Nandagam, Mathura – Uttar Pradesh
20. Kokilavan, Mathura – Uttar Pradesh
21. Bhandirvan, Mathura – Uttar Pradesh
22. Mansarovar, Mathura – Uttar Pradesh
23. Soron Ghat, Ataha – Uttar Pradesh
24. Chitrakut, Allahabad – Uttar Pradesh
25. Ayodhya, Faizabad – Uttar Pradesh
26. Naimisharanya, Situpur – Uttar Pradesh
27. Kashi Shri Purshottamdas House, (Banaras) – Uttar Pradesh
28. Hanuman Ghat, (Banaras) – Uttar Pradesh
29. Harihar, (Hajipur) – Bihar
30. Janakpura, (Hajipur) – Bihar
31. Gangasagar, Kolkatta – West Bengal
32. Champaranya, (Raipur) – Chhattisgarh
33. Champaranya, (Raipur) – Chhattisgarh
34. Jagannath Puri, Vijaya Nagar – Orissa
35. Pandharpur – Maharashtra
36. Panchavati, Nasik – Maharashtra
37. Panna Nirsingh, Machalipattam – Andhra Pradesh
38. Lakshmana Balaji, Tirumalai – Andhra Pradesh
39. Shri Rangji, Trichi - Tamil Nadu
40. Vishnu Kanchi, Kanchi Varam – Tamil Nadu
41. Setu Bandh, Rameshvar – Tamil Nadu
42. Malayachal Mountain, Koimbatur - Karnataka
43. Lohagash, Goa – Konkan
44. Tamraparni River, Ninevelly – Tamil Nadu
45. Krishna River, Wadi Junction – Andhra Pradesh
46. Pampasarovar, Hubali – Andhra Pradesh
47. Padmanabhaji, Trivendrum - Kerala
48. Janardanji, Varkali – Kerala
49. Vidya Nagar, Humpi – Karnataka
50. Trilokbhanji, Totadri Mountain – Tamil Nadu
51. Totadhi Mountain, Nanguneri – Tamil Nadu
52. Darvasenji, Ramnad – Tamil Nadu
53. Tapi River, Surat – Gujurat
54. Bharuch, Bharuch – Gujurat
55. Morbi, Machchhu River – Gujurat
56. Navanagar, Jam Nagar – Gujurat
57. Khambhaliya, Jam Nagar – Gujurat
58. Pindatarak, Jam Nagar – Gujurat
59. Mulgomati, Dwarka – Gujurat
60. Hari Kund, Dwarka – Gujurat
61. Shri Gopi Talaiya, Dwarka – Gujurat
62. Shankhoddhar, Bet Dwarka – Gujurat
63. Narayana Sarovar, Kutch – Gujurat
64. Junagarh Damodar and Ravati Kund, Gujurat
65. Prabhas Patan, Veraval – Gujurat
66. Shri Madhavapur, Keshod – Gujurat
67. Gupta Prayag, Una – Delavada – Gujurat
68. Trigardi, Ahmadabad – Gujurat
69. Naroda, Ahmadabed – Gujurat
70. Godhra, Panch Mahal – Gujurat
71. Kheralu, Mehasana – Gujurat
72. Siddhapur, Mehasana – Gujurat
73. Gomati Kund, Ujjaini – Madhya Pradesh
74. Pushkar, Ajamer – Rajasthan
75. Kurukshetra, Thaneshwar – Uttar Pradesh
76. Ram Ghat, Hardwara – Uttar Pradesh
77. Badrinath Ashram, Uttaranchal
78. Kedarnath, Himachal Pradesh – Uttar Pradesh
79. Vyasahram, Badrinath – Uttar Pradesh
80. Himachal Mountain, Kedarnath – Uttar Pradesh
81. Vyasa Ganga, Hrishikesh – Uttar Pradesh
82. Shri Mudrachal, Hrishikesh – Himachal Pradesh
83. Adel, Allahabad – Uttar Pradesh
84. Charanat, Meerajpur - Uttar Pradesh

In addition to the 84 principal bethaks of Shri Vallabhacharya spread across India (see map below) there are also 28 bethaks of Shri Gosainji, 4 bethaks of Shri Girdharji, 1 bethak of Shri Balkrishnaji, 1 bethak of Shri Raghunathji, 1 bethak of Shri Ghanashyamji, 13 bethaks of Shri Gokulnathji, 7 bethaks of Shri Hariraiji and 5 bethaks of Shri Damodardas Harsaniji.

Geographical Scope of Shri Vallabhacharya's Bethaks

Chapter Eight

Writings

An overview of Shri Vallabhacharya's works

This chapter provides a brief overview of Shri Vallabhacharya's writings, their content, their inspiration, and their significance to the followers of Pusti-Marg.

Shri Vallabhacharya accepted the *four fundamental sacred texts*, namely, the Vedas (or the Upanishads), Bhagvad-Gita, the Brahm-Sutras, and the Bhagvatam as authority (see Prof Bhatt, G.H. [reference 7]). It is understood that these works were ordered in such a way that any doubts or further exposition required of the preceding work are removed in the subsequent one, so that for example, doubts in Vedas are removed through the Bhagvad-Gita, those in the Bhagvad-Gita are removed through Brahm-Sutras, and those in the Brahm-Sutras in the light of the Bhagvatam. Furthermore, the Upanishads (Vedas) and the Brahm-Sutras may be considered as one group, since Brahm-Sutras may be seen as a commentary on the Upanishads. Similarly, Bhagvad-Gita and the Bhagvatam as another group, since Bhagvatam may be considered a commentary on the Bhagvad-Gita.

In addition, despite the texts belonging to different "groups", none-the-less attempts have been made to show that Bhagvatam really explains all the points arising in Brahm-Sutras; in fact every sutra in the latter finds correspondence in the Bhagvatam, and so there is an overall harmony between these two sacred texts. These texts are therefore considered as the highest authority in philosophical terms.

Writings

In the Pusti-Marg, or the Suddhadvaita system, the Bhagvatam, the philosophical and literary classic spoken by Shri Vyasa, which contains the lilas of Shri Krishna, is considered to be of very great significance and strongly emphasises Pusti, or divine grace, as the most important means of enjoying the highest bliss. It is held in the highest esteem, and Shri Vallabhacharya is known to have recited it in the majority of the 84 Bethaks. Indeed, he also wrote the famous commentary on the Bhagvatam, called Shri Subodhini, and this is briefly discussed later.

Shri Vallabhacharya's work as an author is seen as very significant particularly for his sharp intellect and profoundly original thinking. His works - both small and large - show a sense of authority, objectivity and incisiveness, owing to his complete conviction - possibly born of inspiration from God - that what he writes is absolute truth. Even amongst the great acharyas, in his writings, Shri Vallabhacharya undeniably displays extraordinary originality and independence of mind, and was undoubtedly one of the greatest intellects that India has known. While being profoundly intellectual, his life was centred on Bhakti. He was humble in nature, despite his position, and as can be seen in the biographical accounts of his disciples, he was a fatherly figure. He was conscious at all times of having been entrusted with a divine mission, and this is reflected in his works.

Shri Vallabhacharya wrote a number of works as commentaries and others as independent writings. Brief summaries of most of his works are provided below [(*)].

1. **Anubhasya.** This is a commentary on the Vedanta as defined in the Brahm-Sutras of Badarayana Vyasa. The text provides the explanations of the Upanishads from the point of view of Brahmavada or Suddhadvaita philosophy. The sections up to Adhyaya III, Pada II, Sutra 34 were written by Shri Vallabhacharya and the rest were completed by Shri Vitthalnathji, his younger son. To undertake such a task is no ordinary activity, and in fact the writings of Shri Vallabhacharya afforded him the title of Acharya, and a place among the 4 Great Acharyas – the very highest religious

(*) For further details see Parekh, Manilal C. [reference 30], Barz, Richard [reference 5], Bhatt, B.K. [reference 6], Manohar, Shyam [reference 22] and Shyamdas [reference 48].

teachers in India. Although the other Acharyas preceded Shri Vallabhacharya in writing commentary on the Brahm-Sutras, Shri Vallabhacharya felt it necessary to give the true interpretation and view of the Vedanta. This work, in turn, has given rise to a further substantial volume of literature in the form of commentaries. The doctrine of Brahmavada by the leading authority Shyam Manohar is presented in the Brahmavada chapter. (See also Shah, J.G. [reference 36])

2. **Tattva-Dipa-Nibandha** or the Light of Knowledge. This forms an important part of the Independent writings consisting of a sequence of sutras - pithy aphorisms - in a condensed form. Shri Vallabhacharya also wrote Prakash - a commentary on this book, divided into three sections; firstly Sastratha prakarana, which expands on the Bhagvad-Gita; secondly Sarvanirnaya, which inter alia emphasises the importance of bhakti, devotional worship without any desires or expectation; and thirdly Bhagavatartha prakarana, which provides analysis on Shrimad Bhagvatam - this is in addition to his commentary on Shri Bhagvatam, called Shri Subodhini. In the Tattva-Dipa-Nibandha Shri Vallabhacharya successfully harmonises the Scriptures using the Bhagavad Puranas as his central theme, and conveys in a very simple and effective way his thesis on the devotion and seva to Krishna. Subsequently Purshottamarai also wrote a commentary referred to as Avaranabhanga. For further insight refer to the translation of the first part of the original text concerning the meaning of scripture in Parekh, Manilal C. [reference 30]. Below is an English translation from Parekh, of a selection of the sutras, which succinctly amplify Shri Vallabhacharya's thesis. (The spellings here may differ from those used elsewhere in this book, since they are taken directly from Parekh's translation).

   4. *There is but one Scripture, viz., the Song Celestli (the Bhagawad-Gita) sung by the son of Devaki, there is one God, the son of Devaki; there is but one Mantra (holy formula), viz., His names, and there is but one seva (Service or worship) viz., His service.*

7. *The Vedas, the words of Sri Krishna (the utterances of Krishna Himself in the Gita), Vyasa-Sutras and the Samadhi-Bhasha (personal experiences related in ecstatic and inspired language) of Vyasa (in the Bhagavata), these are the authoritative Canon of Scripture.*

8. *Of these four, each succeeding Scripture is meant to remove the doubts springing from the preceding one. Whatever other books are not contrary to these are authoritative, and whatever is contrary to them is never to be accepted as authority.*

11. *In the first part of the Vedic Scripture, God is (seen) in the form of the Yagnas (Sacrifice); in the second (the Upanishads) He is in that of Brahman; in the Bhagavata Gita is described as the Incarnate Saviour Krishna.*

14. *The salvation that is nirguna (free from such qualities as Satva, Rajas and Tamas) is attained only by such service, whereas the salvation that is saguna is attained by the worship of other gods. Even by Knowledge (as given in the Upanishads) one attains only Satvic salvation and Jivan-Mukti. If however the man of knowledge worships Krishna, there is none greater than he.*

42. *The love with a full knowledge of the glory of God, which is besides, well established and surpasses all other kinds of love, is called Bhakti. This alone gives salvation.*

43. *God is in five forms, in twelve forms and in ten forms also; in the same way He manifests Himself in a hundred, thousand and infinite forms. He is the one in all, He is equal (in all), without any defects, perfect in His holy attributes in everything, and much to be praised.*

45. *By knowing Him, one attains final freedom after destroying his Avidya (nescience). Vairagya (detachment from the world), Samkhya, Yoga, Penance and Devotion to God - this is the five-fold Vidya (gnosis).*

49. *Therefore leaving everything (all reliance on places and times), and having firm faith in God, one must worship God by means of hearing etc., (the nine-fold Bhakti); one attains true Gnosis thereby and becomes free.*

71. *Brahman is infinite in form, is motionless, motionful, the support of contrary qualities and unknowable by human reason.*

72. *Brahman causes delusion (in the mind of souls) by manifesting Himself in various ways through His presence and absence. He is invisible to the powers of the senses, but is visible through His will.*

91. *In the indivisible Advaita (Monism) all is Brahman, and there is no distinction. The distinction appears only in the distinction-making intellect, but in reality they do not exist.*

92. *Brahman being the material (cause of all), no difference is possible. The difference, being due only to the necessity of language, cannot arise in reality.*

3. **Shri Subodhini.** This is one of his greatest achievements. It forms part of his Commentary works on Books I, II, III, X, and the first four chapters of the XIth Book of Shrimad Bhagvatam. It is held in the highest esteem, in revealing the beauty and glory of this epic work. It concludes with a fascinating insight into the beauty relating to the Venugita (the Flute Song), the Rasalila section and the Bhramara Gita (the Bee Song).

   By way of background, this work is dearest to Shri Vallabhacharya's heart, as it is a form of God Himself, and can be understood and realised by those with pure heart and free from wordly desires. The followers of Bhagavata, called Mahabhagavata by Shri Vallabhacharya, are only those who are devoted entirely to God, theirs is the true bhakti, and such devotion is the natural atmosphere of the soul. (See Parekh, Manilal C. [reference 30])

   Shri Vallabhacharya wrote Subodhini upon return from his pilgrimage to Jagannath Puri, where he stayed with Madhava Bhatt, one of the 84 disciples, who wrote proficiently and so served as scribe to Shri Vallabhacharya. After completing the first three books, Shri Vallabhacharya received a command from Krishna to end his missionary work on earth, and retire to his abode. However he continued to write, but, it is understood, due to lack of time he proceeded to his commentary on book X which he considered the most important - a form of Krishna, revealing his lilas. After completing book X and part way through XI he could no longer resist Krishna's call, and returned to his abode. The way in which this commentary was written demonstrates the importance placed upon it by Shri Vallabhacharya.

4. **Patravalambana.** Shri Vallabhacharya wrote this in bullet points or folios in order to silence the pandits of the Purvamimamsa School and Mayavadins. It is said that these folios were found hanging on the door of Lord Visvanatha's temple in Banaras and hence the name *Patravalambana.* In these writings Shri Vallabhacharya also provided harmony between Purva and Uttar mimamsas, with single spiritual science, teaching the way of God realisation. (For further insight see Manohar, Shyam [reference 19])

5. **Jaimini Sutra.** Shri Vallabhacharya wrote this bhasya on Purva Mimamsa, but it is understood to be incomplete, the only commentary available on the bhasya includes discussion on the first sutra (see Manohar, Shyam [reference 20]). The Purva Mimamsa and Uttar Mimamsa form part of the six schools of Hindu Philosophy, as explained in the *Study Notes*. Both enquire into the Vedas, the former deals with *dharmas* and *karmas*, ritualistic and other duties of the Veda follower, and the latter deals with the Upanishads or the knowledge aspect of the Vedic scripture.

6. **Shodas Grantha.** Shri Vallabhacharya wrote a composition of sixteen works, which became known as the Shodas Grantha. These are short and succinct works and are very helpful in understanding the Pusti-Marg philosophy as well as the practical measures one should take in order to follow it. Although they were written at different times, often arising from different needs of the Vaishnavas, there is a single thread of devotional spirit throughout all sixteen works. These are the most popular of Shri Vallabhacharya's writings

and many of them are recited daily in countless homes throughout the world. A brief description of each is provided as follows:

i. ***Yamunashtak.*** Once, Shri Vallabhacharya travelled with his sevaks to a desolate Gokul, and arriving at a large forest explained to them, that it was in this very place that Lord Krishna performed his childhood lilas. When they then crossed the Yamuna river, Shri Yamunaji appeared to them. It was here, at the age of fourteen, that Shri Vallabhacharya composed Shri Yamunashtak, and sang the famous Yamunashtak as a eulogy to Shri Yamunaji, which symbolizes a continuous flow of love for Lord Krishna.

   This text stands in whole-hearted praise of Yamunaji, who is Krishna's most beloved. Yamunaji is the source of all divine powers that increases a bhakta's love for Krishna, and transforms the nature of bhaktas so as to enable them to be fit for Krishna's loving service. It is through Shri Yamunaji's grace that a bhakta receives the ability to meet Krishna. It is also said that Ganga, after merging with Yamuna, too became beloved to Krishna and was also able to give devotional powers to those who worshiped her.

Shri Yamunaji

Shri Yamunaji is the daughter of Surya (Sun) and sister of Yam. She is a symbol of Mukti, and is the principal female deity of Pusti-Marg. She is also known as Kalindi, from Mount Kalindi, the source of the Yamuna river, and thus of Shri Yamunaji in her adhidaivika form. She emerged from the heart of Suya Narayan and came to earth to bless bhaktas in order to increase their bhakti bhava.

Shri Yamunaji is revered in three divine forms - *Adhibhautik*, or the materialistic form of river that flows in Mathura, Vrindaven, Gokul, - *Adhyatmika*, or the spiritual form, which grants boon and washes away the sins, - *Adhidaivika*, or the transcendental form, the real form of Shri Yamunaji as one of the maidens of Shri Krishna, experienced by the divine grace of the lord. It is this Adhidaivika form, in which she carries garlands of lotus in her hands for Lord Krishna, as in the picture on the previous page. The concept of the three divine forms is further explained later in Siddhantamuktavali.

Today, countless bhaktas visit the Yamuna river near Mathura, in India's Uttar Pradesh region, and bathe in the river to have their sins removed. Countless bhaktas also sip drops of Yamunaji's waters to have their bodies cleansed and become beloved to Krishna. Daily, in thousands of homes, the Yamunashtak is recited, with deep affection, by bhaktas whilst performing Krishna seva.

Below are the verses of the Yamunashtak, as translated by Shyamdas [reference 48]:

> *I joyfully bow to Shri Yamunaji, the giver of all divine powers. Her expansive sands shine brightly like the lotus feet of Lord Krishna. Flowers from fresh forests on Her banks mingle with Shri Yamunaji and make Her waters fragrant. Both humble and assertive Gopis worship Shri Yamunaji well. She contains the beauty of Krishna. (1)*

Appearing from the heart of Lord Narayan, Shri Yamunaji cascades from the summit of the Kalindi mountain with brilliance. She descends the rocky slopes with dalliance, Her waters roaring as She appears to be swaying in a lovely swing. Glories to Shri Yamunaji, the daughter of the sun, who increases the bhakta's love for Mukunda. (2)

Shri Yamunaji has come to earth for its purification. Like the Gopis serve their beloved Krishna, Shri Yamunaji is served by the many songs of the peacocks, parrots, swans and others. Her waves are Her arms and Her pearly bangles are Her sands. Her banks are her hips. Bow to this beautiful Yamuna, the fourth and foremost beloved of Krishna. (3)

Embellished with countless virtues, Shri Yamunaji is praised by Shiva, Brahma and others. Her hue is always the colour of dark clouds and She fulfils the wishes of Dhruva and Parasha. At Her banks by the pure city of Mathura, She is surrounded by the Gopis. O Yamunaji, You have taken the shelter of Shri Krishna, the ocean of grace. Bring joy to my heart. (4)

Only when Ganga merged with You, O Yamunaji, did She become beloved to Krishna and only then was Ganga able to give all devotional powers to those who worship Her. If there is anyone who can come close to You, it would be Your co-wife Shri Laxshmi. May You remain forever in my heart Kalindi, Beloved of Hari, Destroyer of the strifes of this age of Kali. (5)

Obeisances to You forever, Shri Yamunaji. Your story is most amazing. Those who sip Your waters are never tormented by Yama, the God of retribution, for how could He ever harm the children of His younger sister, even if they are bad? Those who worship You become beloved to Hari just like the Gopis. (6)

By being near you may my body be divinely transformed and renewed. Then it will not be at all difficult to love Krishna. This is why I cherish you. Ganga was praised in the world only after She joined You and grace-filled souls only worship Ganga after she has met You. (7)

Who is capable of praising you, Krishna's beloved Shri Yamunaji, co-wife of Laxshmi? If worshipped in conjunction with Hari, Shri Laxshmi can at best award the bliss of liberation. Your story, however, is far greater, for Your entire body is comprised of the beads of sweat that have dropped from Shri Krishna as He joins with the Gopis. (8)

O Yamuna, Daughter of the sun! Those who joyfully recite this eight-fold praise have all of their impurities removed and love Krishna, the Giver of liberation. Through You all devotional powers are attained and Shri Krishna is pleased. You transform the nature of your bhaktas, says Vallabh, Beloved of Hari. (9)

ii. ***Siddhantamuktavali***. Shri Vallabhacharya wrote the Siddhantamuktavali, sometimes referred to as the Necklace of Doctrine, where he expounds the three types of divine services or seva and asserts Krishna as the Supreme Lord. The three types of seva are Tanuja, through body or physicality, Vittaja, through riches or material and finally Manasi, through the mind where the devotee becomes totally immersed in God. The latter is the most difficult to attain.

By way of an example Shri Vallabhacharya considers a man who goes to the bank of the sacred Ganga river, and views it from the following three perspectives. (i) as a physical stream of water, this is *adhibhautika*, or a material form (ii) he enters the Ganga as a place of pilgrimage which will purify him of his sins, this is *adhyatmika*, or seeing the Ganga as a spiritual form (iii) he praises Ganga as a bhakta of the Ganga, without thought of his own benefit and through the grace of Krishna, and thus he realises the *adhidaivika*, or divine form of the Ganga, non-separate from her waters, yet still distinct. Similarly there are three attitudes towards Supreme Bhagavan Shri Krishna. One sees the physical universe, or *jagat*, which is the *adhibhautika* form of Krishna, realised through own ability, reason, meditation; one concentrates with mental and physical powers upon the impersonal absolute entity, which is the *adhyatmika* manifestation of Krishna; and finally one realises, through the grace of Krishna, the full and complete *adhidaivika* form, which immeasurably exceeds the other forms. This three-fold perspective of Shri Vallabhacharya is prevalent even today when viewing life from the Pusti-Marg standpoint. (See Barz, Richard [reference 4]). In slokas 10 and 11 Shri Vallabhacharya also talks about the nature of creation (see translation by Shyamdas [reference 48]) *'... it has been spoken of as three-fold with Brahma, Vishnu and Shiva as its controlling Deities. Brahman's presiding Deity is distinct from Brahma, Vishnu and Shiva and is known as Hari or Shri Krishna Himself (sloka 10). For attainment of worldly desires only Brahma the creator or other bona fide devas should be resorted to. Without a doubt, one's own Inner Self is Krishna and He is filled with Perfect joy.'* (sloka 11). Siddhantamuktavali also provides an explanation on theism revealed in the Shrimad Bhagvatam, with the deity being Shri Krishna.

iii. ***Pusti-Pravaha-Maryada.*** This book explains that the three paths - Pusti, the grace, Pravaha, the mundane flow or endless drift, and Maryada, the lawful limitation - are all different due to the inherent differences in the souls which correspond in action, progress and the goals they reach. Shri Vallabhacharya describes the three types of devotees, and the rewards that can be achieved by each of them. (For further insight see Manohar, Shyam [reference 18])

iv. ***Balabodha.*** When one of the '84 Vaishnavas', Shri Narayan Kayastha, asked Shri Vallabhacharya for a way out of the worldly pains and pleasures and a means to concentrate on the lotus feet of Krishna, Shri Vallabhacharya taught him

Balabodha. When the soul becomes truly selfless its 'ahanta', egoism, and 'mamta', idea of possession, are removed and it is re-established in its original state. The text uses the principle of dichotomy to compare and contrast different vehicles and leads, by process of elimination, to the worship of Vishnu for the attainment of liberation. It emphasises the importance of self-dedication, and is primarily aimed at persons of pure heart, ignorant of their material wealth, and possessing a child-like innocence.

v. ***Siddhanta Rahasyam.*** In this work Shri Vallabhacharya describes the vow of dedication, consisting of two steps, the Saranagati mantra and the Brahma Sambhandh mantra. Shri Vallabhacharya had serious concerns about how divine souls can achieve the Lord during the impure age of kali.

Shri Krishna himself, at midnight on the eleventh day of the bright half of the month of Shravana, instructed Shri Vallabhacharya, by the banks of the Yamuna river in the sacred town of Gokul, to initiate divine souls into the Pusti--Marg by means of the Brahma Sambhandh mantra, through which a devotee dedicates himself, together with all his belongings and relationships, to Krishna. Furthermore after the initiation, the natural impurities, as well as impurities relating to time, place, association and physical contact, are considered void. The divine souls should then perform all activities by first offering them to the Lord.

vi. ***Navratna***. Shri Vallabhacharya composed Navratna, or the 'Nine Jewels' for his disciple Govinda Dube, in order to remove the anxiety that was preventing him from carrying out Krishna seva. He explains and emphasises that a devotee should not be worried or upset or have any anxiety over any day-to-day concerns since it conflicts with the vow of dedication, Brahma Sambhandh, and shows a distrust in God. The recitation of this text helps the devotees to focus and concentrate on the devotional element and worship of the Lord.

vii. ***Antah-Karana-Prabodha.*** This is a treatise written by Shri Vallabhacharya to himself in order to console *himself* because he twice decided to delay the request by Shri Krishna to leave this world and return to his divine abode, and instead decided to complete the Subodhiniji, his commentary on Shri Krishna's lilas as depicted in Shrimad Bhagvatam. Only after the third request from Shri Krishna, when he could no longer resist, did he decide to retire to his divine abode. Shri Vallabhacharya reflects on his subtle relationship with Lord Krishna, and whilst being critical of himself for not following the Lord's command initially to leave this world, it does show that a devotee should become free of any earthly concern.

viii. ***Viveka-Dhairya-Asraya.*** In this treatise Shri Vallabhacharya explains the terms Vivek - wisdom, Dhairya - perseverance and Asraya - refuge, the three integral qualities to create and maintain firm devotional sentiments in Shri Krishna. Vivek is the realisation that all happenings are due to the Lord's will. Dhairya is enduring the three-fold physical, mental and spiritual misery during a lifespan, and Asraya is the realisation that the Lord is the sole refuge in every situation and condition. These qualities are essential and provide a practical guide to deal with obstruction in our day-to-day life in order to perform seva without a false sense of ownership.

ix. ***Chatussloki.*** Shri Vallabhacharya composed Chatussloki for Rana Vyasa, one of the '84 Vaishnavas'. It establishes, in four succinct verses, the most important duty for an ideal follower of Pusti-Marg. The verses call for the Lord of Vraja, Krishna, to be served without any anxieties and with loving affection and emotions.

Shyamdas [reference 48] explains this very well: each verse provides a grace-filled interpretation of *dharma*, *wealth*, *desire*, *and liberation*. "His worship is our dharma and our wealth is Krishna Himself, our desires are fulfilled when He lives in the heart and always to serve and remember Him is liberation."

Daily in thousands of homes, the Chatussloki is recited, with affectionate emotions, by bkaktas whilst performing Krishna seva.

x. ***Krishnasraya.*** This work arose from Shri Vallabhacharya's association with one of the '84 Vaishnavas', called Bula Mishra. Even after Bula had seen the Lord, he still possessed true humility, which in itself is very important, and Shri Vallabhacharya accepted him as his disciple and taught him Krishnasraya. In this writing Shri Vallabhacharya explains that even in the most adverse conditions that prevailed in India at the time, some five hundred years ago, refuge should be sought in Krishna. He goes on to explain that in the face of hypocrisy, holy sites turn into iniquitous places with the harassment of innocent people, and all paths aimed at the development of spiritual nature become obstructed, but in these very conditions Krishna is the only shelter. Even today it is still recited by vaishnavas during daily seva to help establish total refuge in Krishna.

xi. ***Bhaktivardhini.*** Shri Vallabhacharya composed Bhaktivardhini, an essential text on how to increase bhakti or devotion, originally written for Purushottam Joshi, one of the '84 Vaishnavas'. The writings, consisting of 11 verses, explain how to attain love for Krishna, how to attain divine attachment to Krishna, and ultimate obsession for Krishna. There are two kinds of devotion - Sadhna Rupa (nine-fold devotion) and Sadhya Rupa (expressed through love). There are three phases in the development of devotion: *sneha*, *asakti*, and *vyasana* and in the latter the bhakta is completely immersed in Krishna, who in turn showers his grace so that the bhakta can reach the ultimate state. The three phases may develop as follows. The bhakta starts out living in his own family and carrying out his own day-to-day worldly activity, whatever it may be, but already no longer has attachment to his family or activity since both have already been dedicated to Krishna, as part of the Brahma Sambhandh initiation. By following the nine-step devotion path (of hearing devotional subjects, remembering, singing the praises of the Lord, and so on) thereby achieving loving sentiments towards Krishna, eventually the love or *sneha* for Krishna will begin to grow to the point where it will overshadow the worldly activity and family concerns. These will therefore, no longer distract the bhakta from the complete absorption in and devotion to Krishna, and this complete absorption is referred to as *asakti*, the state of being detached from worldly ties. Subsequently the bhakta reaches the state of *vyasana*, where Shri Vallabhacharya uses the term in an alaukika or spiritual sense, when the love for Krishna totally overwhelms the bhakta, and this is the highest point of love that a bhakta can attain with the grace of the Lord. In this state of vyasana, the bhakta achieves one of the three rewards of perfect seva: either, (i) the eternal experience of the *lila* of Shri Krishna in Goloka as a *sakha* of Shri Krishna, or (ii) union into the divine being of Shri Krishna in Goloka to be manifested by him in his lila, or (iii) the ability to be a non-human being, or inanimate entity in Goloka so as to witness the eternal lila. This is the way by which the human jiva, by the grace of Shri Krishna, achieves the true, alaukika, eternal world in Goloka. (See Barz, Richard [reference 5] which provides further details. Also see writings of Shyam Manohar for further insight).

xii. ***Panchapadyani.*** Here Shri Vallabhacharya explains different types of listener. The listening to devotional elements forms one of the main aspects of Bhakti. Starting with the most inspired, listeners or bhaktas may be described as follows.

- minds and hearts are totally absorbed into Krishna-Rasa, the devotion of those perfectly focused on Krishna, is undisturbed by location, time, wealth, occurrence, mantra, or karma.

- minds and hearts are immersed into Krishna's loving nectar, but listen with underlying desire for liberation or reward

- hearts and minds who know Krishna-Tattwa become temporarily absorbed into divine mood, but often become distracted by worldly attachments.

It should be noted that Shri Vallabhacharya uses the term Krishna-Rasa, in regard to the listeners of highest order, and Krishna-Tattwa in regard to the lowest order. This suggests that, in regards to listening, Shri Vallabhacharya places a Jnani person with tattwa knowledge much lower in rank compared to a devotee with rasa, with deep love and affection towards Krishna. (see Parekh, Manilal C. [reference 30])

xiii. ***Jalabheda***. Similarly to the listeners above, speakers are also categorised. In this rather interesting treatise, analogy is drawn between different types of speakers, including singers, and different types of waters. Shri Vallabhacharya gives an insight into the different nature of speakers who provide disclosures on God. Speakers and water both demonstrate a spectrum of flavours and attributes. He compares, for example, deep water with speakers who can remove the doubts of others, and have profound mind and heart, and he compares them to pure, sweet and nectar-like water. He refers to speakers with little love and knowledge as ponds. He refers to those bhaktas that practice the nine-step devotion path (of hearing, remembering, singing, and so on) thereby achieving loving sentiments to Krishna, as flowing spring water. He compares great devotees such as Shesh, Vyasa, Vayu, Narada, with ocean-like singers who praise Hari with different moods in the vedas. (Shyamdas [reference 48] provides a full English translation.)

xiv. ***Sanyasanirnaya***. Here Shri Vallabhacharya has said that renunciation is only to be resorted to in order to experience the state of separation from Krishna, and for no other purpose. Here the renunciation gives freedom from the bonds of one's home and people; it also removes both pride and false sense of authority. It removes anxiety so that it does not become an impediment in experiencing and loving

Krishna with affection. It gives attainment of proper means to follow the path of Bhakti. It is through the grace of Krishna that Shri Vallabhacharya advocated the pusti form of renunciation; strictly for experiencing the divine love that can be carried out without stepping outside of the home. The treatise was originally written for Naharar Sanyasi, one of the '84 Vaishnavas', who asked Shri Vallabharcharya what renunciation in the path of devotion was.

xv. ***Nirodha-Lakshanani.*** Here Shri Vallabhacharya describes how a devotee can attain a sense of complete withdrawal from daily attachments and continuous attachment to Krishna. In withdrawing from all worldly ties, and renouncing all, one should always sing the praises of God, of perfect joy. Once the mind is withdrawn into God, through it being actively engaged in serving him through different senses, one can attain a level of complete withdrawal.

The short doctrine was originally written for Raja and Madho Dube, the two brothers in the story of the '84 Vaishnavas'. Shri Vallabhacharya explains this in the following way: (See Parekh, Manilal C. [reference 30] and Shyamdas [reference 46]) Firstly, the 'nirodha' of means, is whenever a bhakta's mind is turned towards worldly things he can immediately bring back his senses under control by singing the praises of the Lord. Secondly, the 'nirodha' of fruit, occurs when the mind is continuously thinking about Krishna, so that even while performing worldly duties the mind never leaves the Lord and is constantly focused on Krishna. In this state the bhakta will never suffer the pains of worldly things, and will become blissful in the state of 'satchitananda', full of truth, consciousness and bliss. The bhakta, through the grace of the Lord, experiences the pangs of separation and the joy of union, which Krishna's parents, the Gopis and the other residents of Braja experienced. Shri Vallabhacharya explains further, that through the praising of the Lord, the bhakta experiences supreme bliss that is not even experienced in the hearts of great sages like Sukadevaji. The treatise ends with the explanation that there is no Mantra, Prayer, or Knowledge, or Place of worship greater than Nirodha or complete submission within Krishna.

xvi. ***Sevaphalam***. This last of the sixteen works by Shri Vallabhacharya describes the rewards achievable through the performance of Krishna seva. These rewards are only possible through the divine grace of Krishna. The three types of rewards are (a) *Alaukika Samarthya*: to experience transcendental love and Krishna lila, the highest reward (b) *Sayujya*: the union and the joy of association with Krishna, the second reward and (c) *Sevapeyogi Deha*: attainment of spiritual form that is useful in Krishna's eternal realm, the third reward.

The treatise also clearly explains that worldly anxiety, involvement, and pleasure should be abandoned because it forms a hindrance in performing seva.

This work, as with so many other works of the Shodas Grantha, was originally written for one of the 84 disciples of Shri Vallabhacharya, Vishnudas, a cloth merchant. After being blessed with the sacred initiation mantra, and in order to keep his belief firm in his heart, he asked to know the sublime meaning of the sacred scriptures, and Shri Vallabhacharya subsequently taught him this treatise on the fruit of worship, or Sevaphalam. The translation by Parekh, Manilal C. [reference 30] and Shyamdas [reference 48] offer further insight into the forms of rewards.

Study Notes

The following notes may be of value to students and scholars of comparative philosophy and religion – who have read the previous chapters, and in particular the *Writings* chapter - in understanding Shri Vallabhacharya's philosophy and its place within the broader context of Indian religion.

These brief notes are meant as guidance only. The interested reader is encouraged to pursue these themes further by consulting academic references.

1. Veda, Vedas - The Original Scriptures

These are one of the most ancient sources of vedic literature available, written thousands of years B.C. Divided into four, namely *Rug Veda*, *Sam Veda*, *Yajur Veda*, and *Atharva Veda*. The Veda is also known as *apaurusheya*, meaning 'not from human source' and *Shruti*, meaning 'that which was heard', because it is believed that it is not the work of any human being.

Furthermore each of the four *Vedas* is subdivided into four groups:

The Sahita – the Mantras or Hymns, which praise the different vedic gods.

The Brahmanas - the Explanatory Notes upon the ritual performances of the vedic fire sacrifice.

The Aranyakas - the Forest Treatises, a discussion of the mystical and symbolic meaning of the various elements in vedic ritual.

The Upanishads - the Philosophical Principles, which move further away from vedic gods and ritual, and inquire into the philosophical nature of the universe.

(The interested reader may also like to explore the discussion of the Mantra Vidya, Yagna Vidya, and concept of Brahman, see *Glossary*)

The four Vedas consists of the following:

Rug Veda - includes the Aitareya *Upanishad* and the Kaushitaki *Upanishad.*

Sam Veda - includes the Chandogya *Upanishad* and the Kena *Upanishad.*

Yajur Veda - is a compilation and collection of various Mantras. It has two parts Shukla Yajur Veda and *Krishna Yajur Veda*. The Shukla Yajur Veda includes the Brihad Aranyaka Upanishad and the Isa Upanishad. The *Krishna Yajur Veda* includes the Taittiriya Upanishad, the Katha Upanishad, and the Shvetashvatara Upanishad.

Atharva Veda - includes the Mundaka *Upanishad*, the Prashna *Upanishad*, and the Mundukya *Upanishad.*

2. The Six Systems of Philosophy

The Indian philosophy developed into six systems *Samkhya, Yoga, Nyaya, Vaisheshika, Purva Mimamsa* and *Uttar Mimamsa* or the *Vedanta-Sutras.*

Of these the last one, Vedanta-Sutras, is regarded as the most important, without which the Indian religions and philosophical thought remain incomplete. It compares the tenets of the other systems, and also includes views of other acharyas such as Badari, Ashmarathya, Audulomi and Jaimini. Of these the latter, Jaimini, an acharya of the highest repute, composed Purva-Mimamsa, also referred to as Dharma Sutra, in which he expounded that the pursuit of truth, in the Vedas, is achieved in the performance of Dharma, or sacrifice. However, Badarayana maintained that this view represented only part of the aims of the Vedas.

3. Brahm-Sutras a Study of Vedanta-Sutras

The great sage Badarayana, or Vyasa, further explored the Vedanta-Sutras in his famous work the Brahm-Sutras.

His examination of Aranyakas and the Upanishads, which form part of the Vedas, shows further insights concerning Brahman, as "the Soul", "the Cosmos", "Liberation", and so on, and these thoughts are expounded in Brahm-Sutras.

4. The Schools of Philosophy

The Vedanta philosophy gradually developed into different schools, and the five great philosophers who wrote commentaries on the Brahm-Sutras are:

1. Shankaracharya, whose thesis is *advaita*, Non-Dualism
2. Ramanujacharya, whose thesis is *vishishtadvaita*, Qualified Non-Dualism
3. Madhavacharya, whose thesis is *dvaita*, Dualism
4. Nimbarkacharya, whose thesis is dvaitadvaita, Non-Dualistic Dualism
5. Vallabhacharya, whose thesis is suddhadvaita, Pure Non-Dualism.

Shri Vallabhacharya had reason to believe that his predecessors did not explain the Brahm-Sutras in accordance with its true meaning. He therefore undertook the task of explaining the true meaning of the sastra in his work Anubhasya (see the *Writings* chapter).

Shri Vallabhacharya maintains that everything is real, everything is divine, everything is Brahman, and everything is ultimate truth, and as a consequence the spatio-temporal world and individual souls cannot be unreal or ephemeral. Shri Vallabhacharya explains further that the reason for illusion is due to internal ignorance of man (avidya). (See Sharma, Ishwar C. [reference 39]).

The Vallabhacharya school is a firm platform to realise the Darshan, or vision, as the ultimate truth, and the path, Pusti-Marg, could be practised by anyone from any background, and yet achieve the highest level of self-realisation.

5. In Search of Truth

Indian philosophers often use as the basis of truth or proof (*pramana*) the validity of some or all of the following factors.

a. Shabda or Testimony
b. Pratyaksha or Perception
c. Anumana or Inference
d. Upamana or Analogy
e. Arthapatti or Implication
f. Anupalabdhi or Derivation
g. Sambhavana or Probability
h. Aitihya or History
i. Cheshta or Expectation
j. Pratima or Imagination.

For instance, Shri Madhacharya recognises a) and b), Vaisheshika, b) and c), Samkhya and Shri Ramanujacharya accept a), b) and c). Nyaya recognises a), b), c) and d). Advaita, or Non-Dualism of Vedanta accepts a), b), c) and g).

Shri Vallabhacharya accepts a) - Testimony - as the only proof of knowledge, and the testimony consists of the four sources: the Vedas, the Bhagvad Gita, the Brahm-Sutras, and the Bhagavatam (see *Glossary*) For further details see Sharma, Ishwar C. [reference 39].

6. The Concept of Category in Indian Philosophy

From an academic perspective, Indian Philosophy, and in particular ancient philosophy, can be examined under various categories or concepts, namely *linguistic, aesthetic, universal, logical, ontological,* and *emotion.* Much effort has been made to use these concepts in an attempt to understand the modes of reasoning in the six systems of Indian Philosophy: *Samkhya, Yoga, Nyaya, Vaisheshika, Purva Mimamsa* and the *Uttar Mimamsa* or *Vedanta-Sutras*. Of the six, the last system has received the most attention.

Interestingly, some of the categories seem to arise from cognitive models of Indian culture. In particular, the concept of *bhava* is one of the categories arising from Sanskrit linguistic and philosophical traditions (see Kahrs, Eivind [reference 14]). In fact Kahrs traces its transformation into one of the core categories of Sanskritic thought.

The connection with Shri Vallabhacharya's explanation of *Suddhadvaita* philosophy, which came much later in the 16th century, is that he emphasised and in fact expounded the bhava concept as the central and highest ideal in performing Krishna *seva*, the cornerstone of Pusti-Marg. Furthermore, Shri Vallabhacharya explained that the doctrine of Suddhadvaita Philosphy arises from origins in the Vedas and Upanishads, and is not, in fact, a new concept.

Shri Vallabhacharya wrote the Shodas Grantha, his composition of sixteen works, to illustrate the more pragmatic measures that bhaktas should follow in order to increase bhava and attain divine attachment (see the *Writings* chapter). Today in thousands of homes, Krishna seva is performed with this strong sentiment, or bhava.

Glossary

Included below is a list of terms used throughout this text. The definitions given are relevant to the context in which the terms have been used herein. The majority of these terms are from the Sanskrit language. Some additional definitions, that may provide helpful background information for the reader, have also been included.

Definitions for the majority of the words in *italics* can be found in this glossary.

Acharya:
A teacher.

Atharva Veda
Part of the original scriptures. One of the four *Vedas*, named *Rug Veda*, *Sam Veda*, *Yajur Veda*, and *Atharva Veda*. Believed not the works of any human being. The *Atharva Veda* includes the Mundaka *Upanishad*, the Prashna *Upanishad*, and the Mundukya *Upanishad*.

Bhagavan (Bhagawan, Bhagwan):
God; the Lord.

Bhagvad-Gita, or Geeta:
The "Song of the Blessed Lord": a celebrated scripture in the form of a dialogue between *Krishna* and Arjuna. It is spoken on the battlefield of Kurukshetra, which occurs as an episode in the Mahabharata.

Bhagvatam:
See *Shrimad Bhagvatam.*

Bhakti:
The devotional worship that is given out of pure affection, without any thought or desire for this world, for any other world. See *Nirguna Bhakti.*

Bhava:
An enlightened devotional state of being. A state of being that first develops in the mind and then can be experienced internally and/or as external manifestations.

Bhog:
One of the eight *darshan* of the day. In *Pusti-Marg* devotional routine is symbolised by the eight *darshan* of the day. Also see *Darshan.*

Brahma:
The first created being of the universe; directed by Lord Vishnu, he creates all life forms in the universe.

Brahman:
The word "brahman" in Sanskrit originally meant "power" and specifically referred to the power of prayer or sacrifice to bring about material change in the world (hence the word brahmin for priest). *Brahman* seems to refer to the power that brings about and changes the physical universe. In the *Upanishads*, *Brahman* is not only the principal and creator of all there is, but is also the sum totality of the universe and its phenomena. *Brahman* is:

1) The individual soul
2) The impersonal, all pervasive aspect of the Supreme
3) The Supreme Personality of Godhead
4) The maha-tattva, or total material existence

The term is generally not used as an object of worship, but rather of meditation and knowledge.

Brahma Sambhandh:
Lord Krishna instructed *Shri Vallabhacharya* to initiate divine souls into the *Pusti-Marg* by means of *Brahma Sambhandh*. Through this initiation a devotee dedicates himself, together with all his belongings and relationships, to *Shri Krishna*. To each devotee *Shri Vallabhacharya* gave a deity of *Lord Krishna* in the child-like form of *Thakorji*, and taught them to perform *seva*. Forever after, the devotee will then perform a daily *seva* or 'worship' of *Thakorji*. Only the descendents of *Shri Vallabhacharya* have been entitled to give *Brahma Sambhandh*.

Brahmavada (Suddhadvaita 'Pure Non-Dualism'):
The philosophy where everything is *Brahman* and only *Brahman*. *Shri Vallabhacharya* was one of the greatest philosophers of India, and an advocate of the *Brahmavada*.

Brahm-Sutras:
The sacred text composed by Sage Badarayana. This constitutes one of the six systems of Indian Philosophy. Of the six systems: Samkhya, Yoga, Nyaya, Vaisheshika, Purva Mimamsa and Uttar Mimamsa or *Brahmavada* – the last alone has achieved the most attention in Indian Philosophy. Other names by which it is also known: *The Vedanta-Sutras*, Uttar Mimamsa, Vysa-Sutras, Brahma-Mimamsa, Aupanishada-Mimamsa, Badarayana-Sutras, Tattva-Sutras, Shariraka-Sutras, Shariraka-Mimamsa and Chatur-Lakshani.

Darshan:
To have sacred sight of someone or something, for example, to have sight of *Lord Krishna*. In the *Pusti-Marg*, devotional routine is symbolised by the eight *darshan* of the day. These eight *darshan* are based around the divine child's day as it was in *Vrindavan*. Each *darshan* has a different *bhava* (feeling) associated with it. In order, the eight *darshan* of the day are: *Mangla*, *Sringhar*, Gwala, *Rajbhog*, *Uttaphan*, *Bhog*, *Sandhya* and *Sen*.

Gita
See *Bhagvad-Gita*.

Gokul, Gokula:
The village in Braja (Vraj) in Mathura District of Uttar Pradesh in India where *Lord Krishna* spent his childhood.

Gopis:
Cowherd maiden (eternal consorts of *Lord Krishna*).

Govardhan Mountain:
The sacred mountain in Braja. *Krishna* held it for seven days and nights to protect the bhaktas from Indra, who was sending down a continuous torrent of rain.

Gwala:
One of the eight *darshan* of the day. In *Pusti-Marg* devotional routine is symbolised by the eight *darshan* of the day. Also see *Darshan*.

Krishna:
Lord Krishna brought up by Nanda and Yashoda in Braja.

Krishna Yajur Veda:
From the original scriptures. It forms part of the *Yajur Veda*. It is a compilation and collection of various mantras.

Lilas:
A transcendental pastime or activity performed by the *Lord Krishna*.

Mangla:
One of the eight *darshan* of the day. In *Pusti-Marg* devotional routine is symbolised by the eight *darshan* of the day. Also see *Darshan*.

Narad:
Hindu sage and traveller; devotee of Lord Vishnu.

Nirguna Bhakti:
Being Nirguna or Gunatita means being free from or beyond the influence of all the three earthly attributes of *sattva*, *rajas* and *tamas* and being completely absorbed in the devotion of *Krishna. Pusti-Marg* believes in the *nirguna bhakti*, which is *bhakti* without any object in view and without any desire but accompanied by love. *Shri Vallabhacharya* established and taught the *nirguna bhakti*, which requires rendering divine service to *Lord Krishna*, consciously and with pure heart, without any intention of reward or fruits.

Parayan:
A scripture recital.

Pusti-Marg:
"The Path of Grace": Pusti meaning "grace*", Marg meaning "path". *Pusti-Marg* is the path of dedication, which can be achieved and followed only by the grace of *Lord Krishna. Lord Krishna* instructed *Shri Vallabhacharya* to initiate divine souls into the *Pusti-Marg* by means of *Brahma Sambhandh*. Through many initiations, including the '84 *Vaishnavas'*, *Shri Vallabhacharya* showed individual devotees how to perform *seva* of *Thakorji.* Through his lineage the *Pusti-Marg* principle is followed and *seva* of *Thakorji* is performed in countless households throughout the world today. Also see *Brahmavada, Shri Vallabhacharya.*

Rajasik:
The devotion or *bhakti*, which is compelled by the desire of wanting worldly goods, the object of which is worldly fame. One of the four gunas (*tamasik*, *rajasik*, *sattvic*, *nirguna).*

Rajbhog:
One of the eight *darshan* of the day. In *Pusti-Marg* devotional routine is symbolised by the eight *darshan* of the day. Also see *Darshan*.

Rug Veda:
Part of the original scriptures. One of the four *Vedas*, named *Rug Veda*, *Sam Veda*, *Yajur Veda*, and *Atharva Veda*. Believed not the works of any human being. The *Rug Veda* includes the Aitareya *Upanishad* and the Kaushitaki *Upanishad.*

Sam Veda:
Part of the original scriptures. One of the four *Vedas*, named *Rug Veda*, *Sam Veda*, *Yajur Veda*, and *Atharva Veda*. Believed not the works of any human being. The *Sam Veda* includes the Chandogya *Upanishad* and the Kena *Upanishad.*

Sandhya:
One of the eight *darshan* of the day. In *Pusti-Marg* devotional routine is symbolised by the eight *darshan* of the day. Also see *Darshan*.

Sanyasis:
A person who rejects all mortal attachments.

Sattvic:
Devotion or *bhakti*, the object of which is the destruction of sins, and the pleasing of God by offering him all actions. One of the four gunas (*tamasik*, *rajasik*, *sattvic*, *nirguna*).

Sen:
One of the eight *darshan* of the day. In *Pusti-Marg* devotional routine is symbolised by the eight *darshan* of the day. Also see *Darshan*.

Seva:
The act of pleasing *Lord Krishna* or *Thakorji*. The dedication of one's own body, mind and wealth into the service of *Shri Krishna*. The dedication is performed in one's own home, and the devotee's mind attains an attachment with *Thakorji*. Also see *Brahma Sambhandh* and *Thakorji*.

Shri Gokulnathji (AD 1551 - ~1640):
The fourth son of *Shri Vitthalnathji*. He had a strong and scholarly following including Kalyana Bhatt, the author of Rasikaranjani.

Shri Hariraiji (AD 1647 - 1775):
The illustrious son of Shri Kalyanraiji, wrote the famous Shikha Patra.

Shri Nathji:
Lord Krishna's idol appeared in the form of *Shri Nathji* on the *Govardhan* Hill. Presently the idol is situated at Nathdwara and is visited by many followers, and is one of the key pilgrimage sites in India.

Shri Vallabhacharya (AD 1479-1531):
He established and propagated the principle of *Brahmavada* or the *Suddhadvaita* ('Pure Non-Dualism'), where everything is the form of divinty. *Lord Krishna* instructed *Shri Vallabhacharya* to initiate divine souls into the *Pusti-Marg* by means of *Brahma Sambhandh*. Through many initiations, including the '84 *Vaishnavas'*, *Shri Vallabhacharya* showed individual devotees how to perform *seva* of *Thakorji*. Through his lineage the *Pusti-Marg* principle is followed and *seva* of *Thakorji* is performed in countless households throughout the world today. He was one of the greatest philosophers of India.

Shri Vitthalnathji (AD 1516-1586):
The second son of *Shri Vallabhacharya*, also referred to as Shri Gosainji. He continued his father's work, and the lineage continued through his seven sons.

Shrimad Bhagvatam:
An epic, philosophical, literary classic, and regarded as the sacred text, spoken by Shri Vyasa, which contains the *lilas* of Shri *Krishna*.

Siddhant:
Philosophy or a religious statement.

Sringhar:
One of the eight *darshan* of the day. In *Pusti-Marg* devotional routine is symbolised by the eight *darshan* of the day. Also see *Darshan*.

Subodhiniji:
Shri Vallabhacharya's commentary on *Shrimad Bhagvatam*.

Suddhadvaita:
See *Brahmavada.*

Tamasik:
The devotion or *bhakt*i of a person, who is influenced by anger. One of the four gunas (*tamasik*, *rajasik*, *sattvic*, *nirguna)*.

Thakorji:
A deity of *Lord Krishna* in a child-like form; also see *Brahma Sambhandh*.

Tilaka:
Bindi or *tilaka* (*tilaka* means *red*) is a symbol drawn with clay, ashes (vihuti), or sandalwood on the area in the centre of the forehead (Ajna chakra), as a mark of devotion to the Hindu deities. The *tilaka* has a different design depending on which deity it honours - for example; a tilaka of a "U" shaped mark surrounding a bindu (dot) denotes a follower of *Krishna*.

Tulasi-mala:
A strand of beads made of wood from the sacred tulasi plant.

Upanishads:
The *Upanishads* consists of between 108 and 112 philosophical sanskrit treatises, and are part of the *Vedas* that form the basis of Hindu Religion. The *Upanishads* enter into philosophical discussion upon the nature of this world and the basis upon which it rests. The earliest *Upanishads*

were composed by sages and poets, between 800BC and 400BC. The longest are Brihad Aranyaka and Chandogya, about 100 pages each, while the Isa Upanishad has only eighteen verses. Also see *Veda*.

Uttaphan:
One of the eight *darshan* of the day. In *Pusti-Marg* devotional routine is symbolised by the eight *darshan* of the day. Also see *Darshan*.

Vaishnava:
A devotee of the *Lord Krishna* or Vishnu.

Veda (Vedas, Ved):
The original scriptures. The *Veda* itself is divided into four, named *Rug Veda*, *Sam Veda*, *Yajur Veda*, and *Atharva Veda*. The *Veda* is also referred to as apaurusheya, meaning 'not from human source'. *Veda* is also known as Shruti, meaning 'that which was heard', because it is believed that it is not the works of any human being.
Furthermore each one of the four *Vedas* is subdivided into four groups: Sahita, *Brahmanas*, *Aranyakas*, and *Upanishads*.

Vedanta:
The amalgamation of *Vedas*, the 'anta' means end, hence *Vedanta* either means the 'complete knowledge of *Vedas*', or that which comes at the end of such writings, which are the *Upanishads*. The doctrine of *Vedanta* as expounded by *Shri Vallabhacharya* is *'Suddhadvaita'*, or Pure Non-Dualism, or *Brahmavada*.

Vrindavan, Vrndavan:
The transcendental abode of *Lord Krishna*. It is also called Goloka Vrndavana or Krishnaloka. It is the town of Vrndavana in the Mathura District of Uttar Pradesh, India, where *Krishna* appeared five thousand years ago.

Yajur Veda:
Part of the original scriptures. One of the four *Vedas*, named *Rug Veda*, *Sam Veda*, *Yajur Veda*, and *Atharva Veda*. Believed not the works of any human being. It is a compilation and collection of various Mantras. It has two parts Shukla Yajur Veda and *Krishna Yajur Veda*. The Shukla Yajur Veda includes the Brihad Aranyaka Upanishad and the Isa Upanishad. The *Krishna Yajur Veda* includes the Taittiriya Upanishad, the Katha Upanishad, and the Shvetashvatara Upanishad.

Yamunashtak:
Shri Vallabhacharya was the composer of Shri Yamunashtak. *Shri Vallabhacharya* sang the famous *Yamunashtak* as a eulogy to Shri Yamunaji.

Further information on any of the terms used throughout the text, can be found within the *References* section for relevant literature.

References

The following list of references is not exhaustive and we apologise for any key references we may have omitted.

1. *Aniruddhalalji.* (1998). **Pravesika.** Publisher: Shri Vallabhacharya Trust, Kansara Bajara, Mandvi, Kutch (India).

2. *Aniruddhalalji, Sharad.* (1994). **Pushti-Pravesh-1. And Pushti-Pravesh-2.** Publisher: Shri Purushottam Pushtimargiya Charitable Trust, Junaghadh, Gujarat (India).

3. *Aniruddhalalji, Sharad.* (1995). **Pusti-Path-1.** Publisher: Shri Purushottam Pushtimargiya Charitable Trust, Junaghadh, Gujarat (India).

4. *Barz, Richard.* (1987) **Krishnadas adhikara: an irascible devotee's approach to the divine**, Journal of Comparative Sociology and Religion. 14:35-54.

5. *Barz, Richard.* (1976). **The Bhakti Sect Of Vallabhacharya.** Publisher: Thomson Press (India) Limited, Faridabad, Haryana (India).

6. *Bhatt, B.K.* (1980). **Vallabhacharya.** Publisher: Abul Kalam Azad Oriental Research Institutes, Public Gardens, Hyderabad-4 (India).

7. *Bhatt, G.H.* (1984). **Shri Vallabhacharya and His Doctrines**. Publisher: Shri Vallabha Publications, Baroda, (India).

8. *Bryant, K.E.* (1992) **Three-three-two versus four-by-four: metrical frames for the padas of Surdas**. In R.S. McGregor (ed.) Devotional literature in South Asia: current research, 1985-1988. Papers of the Fourth Conference on Devotional Literature in New Indo-Aryan languages, held at Wolfson College, Cambridge, 1-4 September 1988. Cambridge: Cambridge University Press. 209-24

9. *Burger, M.* (1992) '**The Hindu model of social organisation and the bhakti movement: the example of Vallabha's sampradaya.** In R.S. McGregor (ed.) Devotional literature in South Asia: current research, 1985-1988. Papers of the Fourth Conference on Devotional Literature in New Indo-Aryan languages, held at Wolfson College, Cambridge, 1-4 September 1988. Cambridge: Cambridge University Press. 56-64

10. *Dasgupta, Surendranath.* (1949). **A History Of Indian Philosophy**. Volume IV Indian Pluralism. Publisher: At the University Press, Cambridge.

11. *Dave, S.* (1970) **Dayaram: adhyayan.** Ahmadabad: Anuda Book Depot.

12. *Dwyer, Rachel.* (2001) **The Poetics of Devotion**, Curzon Press, Richmond, Surrey.

13. *Hardy, F.W.* (1983) **Viraha-bhakti: the early history of Krsna devotion in South India**. Delhi: Oxford University Press.

14. *Kahrs, Eivind.* **On Bhave – the ultimate category**, conference proceedings. Thinking inside the box; The concept of a category in Indian Philosophy, Somerville College, Oxford, 10-11 October 2009.

15. *Kinsley, D.R.* (1979) **The divine player: a study of Krsna-lila**. Delhi: Motilal Banarsidass.

16. *Manohar, Shyam.* (1986). **Amrutnu Aachman**. Shri Vallabh Granthmala: Puspa Pahelu. Publisher: Shreekrishnaparn Trust, 15 Darbasha Lane, Off Neapean Sea Road, Bombay-400036. (India).

17. *Manohar, Shyam.* **Antaryamin Akshar And Purushottam**. In the Light Of Vallabha Vedanta. P92-112.

18. *Manohar, Shyam.* (Nov 1986). **Bhakti: Its Experiences and Expressions**. Publisher: Council For the World's Religions, Varanasi (India).

19. *Manohar, Shyam.* (1996). **Commentary On Patravalabnam**. Publisher: Shri Vallabh Vidhyapith-ShriVithaleshprabhucharan A.H. Trust. Vaibhav Co-Operative Society, Poona-Banglore Road, Kolhapur, Maharashtra. (India).

20. *Manohar, Shyam.* (1999). **Purushottamyog.** Publisher: Balkrishna Narandas Sheth. 303, Parekh Plaza, V.P. Road, Vile Parle (West) Bombay-400056 (India). Etc.

21. *Manohar, Shyam.* (1996). **Pushtividhanam**. Publisher: Shri Vallabh Vidhyapith-Shri Vithaleshcharan A.H. Trust, Vaibhav Co-Operative Society, Poona-Banglore Road, Kolhapur, Maharashtra. (India).

22. *Manohar, Shyam.* **Shodash Granth**: Goswami Shyam Manohar. Lal Gebi Darshan, N.S. Road No.4. Vile Parle (West) Bombay-400056. (India). and Etc.

23. *Manohar, Shyam.* (1998). **Shri Balkrishna-Granthavali**. Publisher: Shri Vallabh Vidhyapith-Shri Vithaleshprabhucharan A. H. Trust, Vaibhav Co-Operative Society, Poona-Banglore Road, Kolhapur, Maharashtra (India).

24. *Manohar, Shyam.* (Jan 1992). **Siddhatvachanavali**: Goswami Shyam Manohar. Lal Gebi Darshan, N.S. Road No.4. Vile Parle (West) Bombay-400056. (India). and Etc.

25. *McGregor, R.S.* (1973) **Nanddas: the round dance of Krishna and Uddhav's message.** Translated with an introduction. London: Luzac & Co. Ltd

26. *McGregor, R.S.* (1992) **The padas attributed to Nanddas**. 'In R.S. McGregor (ed.) Devotional literature in South Asia: current research, 1985-1988. Papers of the Fourth Conference on Devotional Literature in New Indo-Aryan languages, held at Wolfson College, Cambridge, 1-4 September 1988. Cambridge: Cambridge University Press 237-46

27. *Neralla, M., et al.* (2002). **Jagad Guru Shrimad Vallabhacharya**. Publisher: Shri Gusainji Charitable Trust, Mumbai-400026 (India).

28. *Parekh, Lallubhai Pranvallabhadas.* (1998). **Shrimad Vallabhacharyaji Jeevan Charitra.** in Gujarati. Publisher: Antar Rashtriya Pustimargiya Vaishnav Parishad, Shri Vallabh Vigayan Prakashan Samiti, Kansara Mahajan Wadi Building, Lohanapara, Rajkot-360001 (India).

29. *Parekh, Lallubhai Pranvallabhadas.* **The Pusti-Marg**. Publisher: Antar Rashtriya Pustimargiya Vaishnav Parishad, 25/31 Lalmani Bhavan, Dr. Atmaram Merchant Road, Bhuleshwar, Bombay-400002 India.

30. *Parekh, Manilal C.* (1943). **Shri Vallabhacharya: Life, teachings and movement, a religion of grace** (Sri Bhagavata Dharma Mission series; v.6). 500p. Publisher: M.C.Parekh.

31. *Parikh, J.M.* (1983) **Sri Pustimargiya Sevaprakas**. Ahmadabad: Shri Lakshmi Pustak Bhandara.

32. *Parikh, Rameshbhai, Prof.* Madhura **Mahaprabhuji**. Publisher: Shri Harsaniji Public Charitable Trust, 'Vrajraj' 31 Shiv Society No. 2 Mahesana-384002 (India).

33. Pusti-Bhakti-Sudha, Vol. V, Nos 2; Vol.VIII, Nos 2.

34. *Sandesara, B.J.* (1981) **Dayaram**. New Delhi: Sahitya Akademi. In series 'Makers of Indian Literature'.

35. *Sargeant, Winthrop.* (1994). **The Bhagavad Gita**. Publisher: State University of New York Press, Albany, ISBN 0-87395-830-6 (pbk).

36. *Shah, J.G.* (1984). **An Introduction to Anubhasya**. Presentation of Shri Vallabhacharya's commentary on Vedanta Sutra of Badranarayan Vyasa. Publisher: Shri Vallabh Publication, Baroda (India).

37. *Shah, J.G.* (1969). **Shri Vallabhacharya, His Philosophy and Religion.** Publisher: Nadiad Pustimargiya Pustakalaya.

38. *Shah, Natvarlal Gokaldas.* (1984). **A Life Of Shri Vallabhacharya.** Publisher: Shri Vallabha Publications, Opp. Surya Narayan Baugh, Raopura Road, Baroda-390001 (India).

39. *Sharma, Ishwar C.* Translator. (1979). **The Vedanta Of Pure Non-Dualism.** Original text by Shri R Kaladhar Bhatt in Hindi, entitled The Heritage of the Philosophical Tradition of Shri Vallabhacharya. (1979). Publisher: A Unilaw Library Book. Donning Virginia Beach / Norfolk. ISBN 0-915442-93-0.

40. *Sharma, Raghunath.* (1992). **Brahmavada The System of Shuddhadvaita Vedanta of Sri Vallabhacharya.** Publisher: Shri Goswami, Manu Bhuvan, Bhagatsinh Road, Vile Parle (West), Bombay-400056. (India).

41. *Shyamdas*, Presentor. (2002, 2003). **252 Vaishnavas**. Part One and Part Two. Originally compiled by Shri Gokulnathji with Shri Harirayji's commentary. Publisher: Pratham Peeth Publication.

42. *Shyamdas*, Translator. (1985). **Ashta-Chhap.** Originally compiled by Shri Gokulnathji. Publisher: Shri Vallabha Publications, Opp. Surya Narayan Baugh. Raopura Road, Baroda-390001 (India).

43. *Shyamdas*, Translator. (1985). **Chaurasi Baithak. Eighty-Four Seats of Shri Vallabhacharya**. Originally compiled by Shri Gokulnathji. Publisher: Shri Vallabha Publications, Baroda (India).

44. *Shyamdas.* (Nov 1997). Magazine 'Hinduism Today' article on **The Path of Grace.**

45. *Shyamdas.* **Pusti Asmita**, Dayaram and Goswamy Shyam Manohar on the teachings of Vallabhacharya.

46. *Shyamdas*, Translator. (1985). **Shri Mahaprabhu Vallabhacharya's 84 Vaishnavs**. Originally compiled by Shri Gokulnathji. Publisher: An International Pusthi Margiya Parishad Publication, Delhi (India).

47. *Shyamdas.* (2004). **The Path of Grace**. Publisher: Pratham Peeth Publication.

48. *Shyamdas*, Translator. (2003). **The teachings of Shri Vallabhacharya**. Translation of Shri Vallabhacharya's Sixteen works. Publisher: Pratham Peeth Publication.

49. *Telivala, M.T.* (1980). **Suddhadvaita Brahmavada**. Publisher: Anand Prakashan Sansthan, Varanasi (India).

50. *Wilson, Dr.* **Hindu Religion.**

Index

A

B

C

D

G

J

K

L

M

N

O

P

S

Y